HEARTBREAK
IS THE
NATIONAL
ANTHEM

HEARTBREAK IS THE NATIONAL ANTHEM

HOW TAYLOR SWIFT REINVENTED POP MUSIC

—

ROB SHEFFIELD

DEYST.

An Imprint of WILLIAM MORROW

HarperCollins books may be purchased for educational, business, or sales promotional use. For information, please email the Special Markets Department at SPsales@harpercollins.com.

FIRST EDITION

Designed by Jennifer Chung

Grainy texture © Xenia800/stock.adobe.com, Polaroid clothespin © Ortis/stock.adobe.com, Polaroid © Graphiste-J/stock.adobe.com, Film reel © 9dreamstudio/stock.adobe.com, Leaves © Pixel-Shot/stock.adobe.com, Paper plane © daboost/stock.adobe.com, Feather © LiliGraphie/Shutterstock

Library of Congress Cataloging-in-Publication Data has been applied for.

ISBN 978-0-06-335131-8

24 25 26 27 28 LBC 5 4 3 2 1

The time of my life: for Sarah ("Long Live"), Sydney ("Tim McGraw"), Allison ("Right Where You Left Me"), Charlie ("Enchanted"), Matthew ("Champagne Problems"), Jackie ("White Horse"), David ("Clean"), Maggie ("Nothing New")

"Is it romantic how all my elegies eulogize me?"

—Taylor Swift, "The Lakes"

CONTENTS

A VERY FAST TIMELINE

1989

Taylor Alison Swift is born in Pennsylvania, on December 13. She grows up on a Christmas tree farm. Absurdly on brand, right from the start.

1992

Younger brother Austin is born, to mother Andrea and father Scott.

2004

The Swift family moves to just outside of Nashville, so Taylor can pursue country music. At fourteen, she signs her first professional songwriting deal, with Sony/ATV.

2005

Taylor plays a gig at Nashville's Bluebird Cafe, singing her original tunes. The first tune she plays is called "Writing Songs About You." She signs her first record deal, with new label Big Machine.

2006

She makes her self-titled debut album with producer Nathan Chapman, during her freshman year of high school. Writes or cowrites all eleven tracks. Her first single, "Tim McGraw," a song she began in math class, reaches number six on the *Billboard* country charts, number forty on the pop chart.

2006–2007

On tour, as opening act for George Strait, Brad Paisley, Rascal Flatts, Faith Hill, and Tim McGraw. (Yes, she plays "Tim McGraw.") Sings George Michael's "Last Christmas" on her *Holiday Collection*. "Our Song" and "Teardrops on My Guitar" become pop crossover hits.

2008

Her *Beautiful Eyes* EP appears in March. Drops her second album, *Fearless*, in October. The hits include "Fifteen," "You Belong With Me," and "Love Story."

2009

Her first headlining tour, for *Fearless*. She plays herself in *Hannah Montana: The Movie*, with Miley Cyrus. At the MTV Video Music Awards in September, she gets interrupted by famous rapper Kanye West, who literally takes the mic out of her hand. Beyoncé wins Video of the Year and brings Taylor onstage. She hosts *Saturday Night Live* in November, with her "Monologue Song." The media talks about her boyfriends.

2010

Fearless wins the Grammy for Album of the Year. She appears in *Valentine's Day*, her first time acting in a movie. She releases *Speak Now*, the first (and last) time she writes all the songs solo. The hits include "Mine," "Mean," and "Back to December." Everybody agrees there's no way she will ever top it. The media talks about her boyfriends.

2011

The *Speak Now* tour. Surprise guests join her for duets: Nicki Minaj, Usher, Hayley Williams of Paramore, T.I., Kenny Chesney, Tim McGraw. Closes the tour with James Taylor, quoting her mom to the crowd: "You were kinda named after him!" She adopts her first cat, Meredith.

2012

Taylor releases *Red*. The hits include "We Are Never Ever Getting Back Together," "I Knew You Were Trouble," and "22." Everybody agrees there's no way she will ever top it. The media talks about her boyfriends.

2013

The Red Tour. Taylor plays the Grammy Awards doing "All Too Well." A male country music DJ in Denver gropes her backstage, during a photo, then later sues her for talking about it. She buys a house in Rhode Island, formerly belonging to infamous heiress Rebekah Harkness.

2014

On *1989*, a drastic sonic change-up, she goes for zippy synth-pop with producers like Max Martin and the up-and-comer Jack Antonoff. The hits include "Shake It Off," "Blank Space," and "Style." Another cat, Olivia.

2015

The *1989* tour. Taylor battles Spotify and Apple Music over royalties for songwriters. Shows up in the gossip columns with her "Girl Squad" of friends, including Karlie Kloss, Lena Dunham, the Haim sisters, and sundry actresses and models. Taylor and then-BFF Kloss appear together on the cover of *Vogue* ("Inseparable, Unstoppable, Adorable"). She appears at the MTV VMAs to give the lifetime achievement award to "my friend Kanye West."

2016

1989 wins the Grammy for Album of the Year. Taylor becomes hugely unfashionable after West releases a song attacking her. A famous reality-TV star calls her a snake on social media. Everybody agrees her reputation is ruined forever.

2017

Reputation drops in November. The single "Look What You Made Me Do" makes people expect an album of celebrity shade, but it turns out to contain nearly all love songs. The hits include "Call It What You Want," ". . . Ready for It?," and "Delicate." She begins a six-year relationship with British actor Joe Alwyn.

2018

The *Reputation* tour, featuring gigantic snakes. Her contract with Big Machine ends, and she signs with Universal Music.

2019

Lover is released in July, with hits like "Lover," "You Need to Calm Down," and "The Man." She announces the Lover Fest tour. Her Big Machine boss sells her catalog to Scooter Braun, Kanye West's manager, with whom she has bad blood. She responds by announcing plans to rerecord her albums. Everybody assumes it's a bluff. She stars in the big-budget Hollywood box-office bomb *Cats*. Another cat, Benjamin.

2020

The documentary *Miss Americana* debuts in January. Taylor announces a new album, with less than a day's notice, in the midst of the Covid-19 pandemic. *Folklore* is her biggest musical surprise yet, full of stark acoustic tales. Does the same thing in December with *Evermore*, saying, "We just couldn't stop writing songs." In November, she debuts *Folklore: The Long Pond Studio Sessions*, playing in an upstate New York cabin with Antonoff and the National's Aaron Dessner.

2021

Folklore wins the Grammy for Album of the Year. Her first rerecorded album, *Fearless (Taylor's Version)*, arrives in May, followed in October by *Red (Taylor's Version)*, both blockbuster hits. *Red*'s "All Too Well," in its expanded ten-minute version, becomes the longest number one hit in history.

2022

She gets an honorary doctorate from NYU and gives the commencement address, telling the graduates, "Learn to live alongside cringe." Dr. Swift speaks at the Tribeca Film Festival, showing her "All Too Well" short film. When *Midnights* drops in October, Taylor has all ten songs in *Billboard*'s top ten. "Anti-Hero" becomes her longest-running number one hit, at eight weeks.

2023

The Eras Tour begins. In April, she announces her split with Alwyn.

Gossip about her single life reaches DEFCON "Blank Space" levels. Two more number one *Taylor's Version* remakes: *Speak Now* and *1989*. "Cruel Summer," a *Lover* deep cut, blows up into a number one hit, four years after it came out.

2024

Taylor invades the NFL, dating Kansas City Chiefs star Travis Kelce. She attends the Super Bowl with Lana Del Rey. Right-wing conspiracists accuse her of a psy-ops plot, rigging NFL games to claim the New World Order. She becomes the first artist in Grammy history to win Album of the Year four times, breaking the record set by Frank Sinatra, Paul Simon, and Stevie Wonder. In April, she releases a new hit, *The Tortured Poets Department*.

OUR SONG IS A SLAMMING SCREEN DOOR

The first Taylor song that ever ruined my day was "Our Song." That's my origin story: the first one I heard, the one that made me a fan, the one that knocked me sideways in the middle of lunch. My ritual in the summer of 2007 was fixing a grilled cheese sandwich and watching the CW's afternoon reruns of the *Clueless* sitcom and *What I Like About You*. They spun pop hits between episodes, but this one made me lunge in from the kitchen. "Our song is a slamming screen door"—what a chorus. I loved every detail—the banjo, the fiddle, her twang when she sings, "It's late and your mama don't know!" But especially that ending, when the girl picks up her guitar and writes her favorite song, i.e. the one she just sang—the music she's been waiting her whole life to hear.

I Googled the song to see who wrote it—I loved the voice, but I was even more curious where this tune came from. It turned out the singer was also the sole songwriter—a rarity in country music at the time. It turned out the songwriter was also the singer. And—

how bizarre—she was just starting out? And only sixteen? Damn. I hoped she might have another great song or two in her.

November 2011: Taylor Swift live, at Madison Square Garden in New York City. The final days of the North American leg of her *Speak Now* tour. My first time seeing her onstage. Since that day I first heard "Our Song," she's written two or three dozen of my favorite songs. She introduces herself with the words, "I was hoping it would be cool with you if I stood here and told you a few of my stories."

By now, Taylor's famous, not merely country-famous. A singer, songwriter, guitar hero, teller of tales, haver of feelings, actress in the flop film *Valentine's Day*. I've raved about her in the pages of *Rolling Stone*. As a six-foot-five dude, I already knew I wouldn't be standing tonight, to avoid blocking the rows behind me, but as soon as I get to my seat, I realize I can't even sit up straight—many of the fans around me are just two or three feet tall. I didn't realize she had this many little kids in her audience. So I scrunch down and marvel. The fans know they're stars of the show, with their homemade costumes, their Lite Brite getups, and more glow sticks than a rave. They wear colored lightbulbs on their heads, full of cat motifs or the number 13, holding signs like "Speak Meow." For most of them, Taylor is the first girl they've seen play a guitar. They're here to see Taylor sing her life, and hear their lives get sung.

She's already the master of every rock-star move, except the one about occasionally dialing it down a notch or two. The opening jangle of Tom Petty's "American Girl"—her walk-on theme—triggers ear-bleeding fan hysteria like I've never heard. The crowd instantly hits ungodly levels of girl-shriek saturation that stays at peak jet-engine volume for the next two hours. The audience is wired to every flutter of her guitar fingers, every catch in her voice. She tells these girls, "Sometimes you need a song that says how you feel."

And she keeps telling them—over and over—that she can see them. "I look into this audience and I see a lot of creativity," she says. "I just remember lying in bed at night when I was a little kid, dreaming about what it might be like to be a singer and get to do what I loved. It looked cool. But it didn't look nearly as cool as what I'm looking at right now. I guess what I'm trying to say is that you look better than a daydream!"

Nobody in the room is holding back, least of all Taylor. Who else has songs like this? The emotionally voracious rock surge of "Long Live"? The whisper-to-a-scream romance of "Enchanted"? The hot-headed pop-punk of "The Story of Us"? The hot-hearted turbulence of "Love Story"? The sinus-exploding doo-wop ache of "Last Kiss"? The defiant outcast solidarity of "Ours"? Nobody, that's who. The archetypal Taylor Swift heroine is the shy girl trying to cop an attitude, talking tougher than she actually is, trying to fake it till she makes it. That's why I relate. I have spent so much of my adult life putting on a brave face, acting like I had it all nailed when my insides were Jell-O. So far, I've mostly listened to her music by myself on headphones. But now I'm hearing her out loud, where she takes the most gauche emotions and amps them up to arena size.

The only moment that leaves me chilly is when she plays a Justin Timberlake tune, my cue to search for a men's room that hasn't been converted for the night. The only one I search for is so sparklingly clean, you could eat breakfast out of the sink.

Every night on this tour, she sings a local tribute song. In Louisiana she just sang Britney Spears's "Lucky"; in DC, it was "Ghetto Supastar" in honor of Mya. She often brings up a hometown hero. In Atlanta, she duetted with T.I., who rapped "Live Your Life" while she sang the Rihanna part. Who will NYC get? None of us guessed right: Johnny Rzeznik, from the Nineties rockers the Goo Goo Dolls, repping Buffalo. They sing "Iris," which Taylor calls "one of the greatest songs ever written." Johnny doesn't seem jazzed to be there, as if he isn't sure this gig is 100 percent the right place for him. Let's just say it: he looks kinda embarrassed. Taylor's a lot more into doing "Iris" for these fans than he is, or they are, but she sells it with gung-ho enthusiasm. I can't blame Johnny for his mixed feelings, but there's something clumny sweet about this cross-generational moment, seeing him face the Taylor fans and sing, "I just want you to know who I am."

I walk out in a joyful haze. I've been a music journalist for a while, gone to a million live gigs, seen all the greats. But I've never seen her like—that level of total commitment, total fan fervor, total connection between audience and performer. For me, it's like my teenage punk all-ages shows where I fell in love with the chaotic slam-dance thrill of live music. But I leave the room even more excited for the future I can already see coming. I can't stop thinking, *I can't WAIT until all these girls grow up and start bands of their own.* So many kids falling in love with music as something they can be a part of. So many young fans hearing Taylor tell them that girls have stories, and these stories deserve telling. They'll learn to play guitar. They'll write their novels, paint their paintings, live their lives. I can't shut up to my friends about it. *Ten years from now, my favorite music will be coming from these girls. The ones who saw this show or heard these songs on the radio, heard this voice tell them, "Drop everything now." They heard her and decided they needed to do it themselves.*

As it turns out, that's exactly what happened.

HEARTBREAK
IS THE
NATIONAL
ANTHEM

PLANET TAYLOR: NICE TO MEET YOU, WHERE YOU BEEN

Nothing like Taylor Swift has ever happened before. There's no parallel to her in history. In 2024, she's at the peak of her fame, her cultural and commercial impact, her artistic powers, her warp-speed work pace. But she's been at this level for eighteen years. This just never happens. Nobody's had a run like this, getting more popular and prolific all the time, still at the top of the game. There's nobody you can compare her to, not even the greats. The Beatles' whole run as recording artists lasted eight years, yet at that point, she was just taking off with *1989*.

There aren't any other stories like Swift's—the world has only one of her, which is probably all the world could take. "Hi, I'm Taylor," she used to say on the Red Tour. "I write songs about my feelings. I'm told I have a *lot* of feelings." You are told this accurately, Taylor.

In the 2020s, Taylor is a cultural obsession. She's the messiest, most fascinating figure in pop music, a red-carpet celebrity whom supposedly everybody knows, the most public of artists, yet also the most deeply weird and mysterious. When she first showed up, she was a teenage girl out to conquer Nashville with a guitar, which she could play, and a Southern accent, which she couldn't play at all. She became America's sweetheart as a country singer, but then swerved into synth-pop and blew up even bigger. At this point, she's the most massive pop sensation since Michael Jackson or the Beatles, her popularity on the rise even when it seems like there's nowhere for her to rise to. She's scored seven number one albums in the 2020s. A global phenomenon. An emotional agent of chaos. An activist in the cause of feminine loudness. An enabler of hyperemotional excess. A born rock star.

By now, she's become the star who embodies pop music in all its maddening contradictions and cultural riddles. Over the years, she will keep experimenting and mutating, always rushing on to her next mistake. She'll reign as the most divisive figure in pop culture. She will make head-spinning artistic shifts nobody expects or even wants. She'll get a stadium full of fans to stand every night and scream, "Fuck the patriarchy!" She will make synth-disco albums and acoustic folk albums. She will decide, for strictly personal reasons, to rerecord her entire catalog, an idea anybody could tell her won't work, except she'll not only get away with it, she'll make each *Taylor's Version* release an event. She will get millions of people around the world to have feelings about a scarf that Maggie Gyllenhaal probably used to mop up some spilled chamomile tea in 2011.

She will be so many different Taylors, way too many, and they'll all want the microphone all the damn time. She will make brilliant moves—or catastrophic gaffes, because that's what rock stars do, giving us facepalm concussions. She'll break up with country music, then get back together. She will break up with being single, then get back together. She will get judged, denounced, laughed at, condemned. (Ignored? That one's not really in the cards.) She will have great ideas and terrible ideas. She will turn some of these terrible ideas into great songs, or vice versa. She will find the drama in any situation, no matter how trivial or ordinary it might seem. She will change how pop music is made, heard, experienced. She will bait. She will switch. She will be a terrible role model for anyone trying to lead a calm and sensible emotional life. She will jump into every feeling with the certainty that it's the last one she'll ever have.

In 2024, it's a cliché to say Taylor Swift *is* the music industry, but it isn't necessarily wrong. Her Eras Tour is such a blockbuster, it's hard to place it into industry perspective—the revenue in 2023 was $1 billion, more than the next two biggest tours (Beyoncé and Bruce Springsteen) put together. In the first half of 2024, *The Tortured Poets Department* was not just the biggest-selling, most-streamed album, it outsold the rest of the year's top ten combined. And five of the top ten were *her* albums. Every time it seems like Taylor Swift has reached the point where she can't get any more popular, she takes another surge, to the point where even a fan has to find it mystifying. How can she keep getting bigger? How can so many people keep hearing pieces of themselves in these songs? There are countless theories to explain her success, yet they all fail. It's not her fashion. It's not her famous boyfriends. It's not her elaborate personal mythology. It's not her role modeling, or lack thereof. It can't be reduced to fashion, trends, lyrics, image, or business sense. She's not a phase that sensitive youth go through and then outgrow. But what is it?

Taylor's always a songwriter before she's anything else, even when it's the last thing anyone wants to notice. But she's always had a unique flair for writing songs in which people hear themselves—her music keeps crossing generational and cultural boundaries, in the most mystifying ways. She sang to her original teen fans, yet she was never willing to stop there—she wanted the world to hear these songs. You could always hear that—she'd studied her idols, learned their tricks, learned how to put her own spin on them. Even as a kid, she had a scholarly sense of music history and a brash sense of her place in it. She set out to write herself (and her audience) into the whole long, gaudy, bloody, messy, crazy story of pop music. But nobody could have predicted how far these songs would travel.

To some, Taylor is a creative genius, a cultural force, a feminist rebel crashing history with her girls-to-the-front energy, with the power to heal sick kittens. To others, she's a selfish, scheming, sniveling bratfiend, a hypocrite whining about feminism and artists' rights just to avenge her petty slights, shrew of all shrews, here to play the victim, slander menfolk, and serve as an all-around one-woman bitch pack symbolizing all that is foul in the sewers of human vanity. A symbol of capitalism, privilege, self-absorption, self-pity, self-indulgence. A flashbulb-chasing vixen collecting celebrity boyfriends as songwriting material. A corrupter of family values. An American idiot. An attention junkie getting up to dance at award shows, making it all about her. A robber-baron plutocrat supervising the corporate takeover of music, under the wing of Big Taylor. A spoiled princess on a throne of evil.

Taylor's hubris, her way-too-muchness, her inability to Not Be Taylor for a microsecond—it's a lot. It's totally understandable that she drives people up the wall. She has never lacked for artistic confidence. She was still a teenager when she took on the story of Romeo and Juliet and decided to *change the plot*. ("I talked to your dad"? Romeo just stabbed Juliet's cousin!) Even as a child, her career drive was so relentless it was scary to behold. On her first national radio interview, in 2006, the host asked, "'I wouldn't be where I am today without . . .' What?" This was a softball. The moment when any rookie knows to thank her parents, for teaching her to follow her dreams. Or God, who makes all things possible. Or her fans, because she couldn't have done it without them, you guys rule.

Taylor doesn't hesitate. "I wouldn't be where I am today without my guitar."

She inspires devotion, hatred, fear, contempt, more shade than a Christmas tree farm in July. You can't fully appreciate her without appreciating the wide range of visceral reactions she brings out in people. It's part of what makes her Taylor—you can always start an argument about her. Many people often find Taylor infuriating and exhausting. So does Taylor Swift.

THERE'S NOTHING LIKE THE FAN COMMUNITY SHE CREATES. I went to three straight nights of the Eras Tour, and I was in the first-night parking lot about ten minutes before someone I'd never met gave me a BETTY'S CARDIGAN friendship bracelet. All three nights were tribal ritual celebrations, with the Swifties dressed to kill: so many Miss Americanas, cowgirls, mirrorballs, a NYU graduation cap and gown, an Eagles tour shirt from the Seventies. (My niece's housemates went as a couple of Wide-Eyed Gays.) I brought extra packs of tissues, which came in handy on Sunday night, when the *Fearless* interlude inspired a few meltdowns in my row. When Taylor began the *Evermore* section with "'Tis the Damn Season," the security guy came over and said, "You the guy with the tissues?" Another couple of fans were having tear-duct emergencies a few rows away, sobbing to me, "I really love this album!" Only at a Taylor show. The woman behind me who responded to the intro of "All Too Well" by dropping to her knees and spending the entire ten minutes sobbing in a fetal position, you are my goddamn hero.

One of the central paradoxes of Taylor Swift—and this woman is nothing BUT paradoxes—is how she writes songs about the tiniest, most secretive agonies, the kind you wouldn't even confess to your friends, except the only way she knows how to process these moments is turning them into louder-than-life stadium scream-alongs. It is so weird to sing "My Tears Ricochet" with sixty thousand people, with Taylor swirling in a goth-priestess gown, leading a funeral procession of black-hooded mourners. The moment when Taylor gets to the almost-hidden line "when I'm screaming at the sky"—and she really does scream it at the sky—was cathartic. No matter how well you know these songs, it's different hearing them in a crowd of blood-hungry Swifties, all here for that communal rapture, that ecstatic release, that catharsis in the dark.

At one point on Sunday night, during the *Midnights* finale, I heard voices and thought the security guard near me was arguing with a fan. It turned out they were just trading friendship bracelets. It was that kind of show. The Eras Tour is a journey through her past, starring all the different Taylors she's ever been, which means all the Taylors that *you've* ever been. Taylor designs each tour to be the best night of your life. But she designed this one to be the best night of *all* your lives, with every era you've ever lived through. It's a celebration of all the holy ground she and her audience have traveled together over the years. There's no experience like being part of that world she creates.

For my little nieces, born in the early 2000s, Taylor was the Beatles times Motown times Bruce Springsteen times Britney times strawberry ice cream. They turned their bedroom walls into fan shrines, covered with photos, lyrics, album covers. When my sister looked at her daughters' rooms, she said, "When I was their age it was all pictures of boys." They devised plans for the night Taylor would babysit them; they were crushed to learn that not all teenage girls babysit. They learned guitar so they could play these songs. They taught me to read the secret codes in the lyrics. But I bombed their Taylor trivia test so abysmally—failed to spell "Wyomissing" right—that I never got the chance for a make-up.

"White Horse" was the song that my toddler niece and nephew, aged three and four, would sing to each other in my parents' backyard. They took turns—one stood on the porch to sing, while the other listened as the audience, cheering and clapping, then they traded places. They had no trouble hearing themselves in this song, as the authentic voice of an older girl, telling her feelings. But they also loved the climb up the porch stairs, the transformative power of becoming the singer, stepping into that imaginary spotlight. To them, that power was built right into "White Horse," and it was theirs to take.

What is Taylor's biggest contribution to the pop music landscape? What makes her different from any other young hustler who ever wanted to rule the world when she grew up? She has taken the pop girl and made her the center of music—not a genre, not a style, not a fad. She reinvented pop in the fangirl's image. In the 2000s, when she began, a young girl writing her own hit songs about her own feelings was rare. Now that's just what pop is.

She's always lived up to "Fifteen," written when she was still south of her twenties, speaking live and direct to her fellow teenage girls, insisting that even the most ordinary girl had a story to tell. Their stories mattered; their secrets were valuable and their friendships real. An entire generation of listeners has grown up in a world where music's biggest star is also the one insisting that every girl has a song in her heart and a right to sing it, and that every girl will improve her life by listening to other girls' songs, even if the only short-term benefit is a sloppy bathroom-line tequila-spilling hug. It's not even strictly accurate to say she crossed over from country to pop, since there wasn't a precedent for the kind of pop star she decided to become, so she had to create something new. What James Taylor said of Joni is true of Taylor: "She's building the canvas as well as she is putting the paint on it." Now we live in a world of Taylor Swifts.

She always went clumsily out of her way to bring those girls into the music, stressing how easy it was. On the Red Tour, she explained her twelve-string guitar to the younger fans. "It has twice as many strings as a regular guitar," she said. "So that's your math for the night."

TAYLOR'S FIRST BIG PUBLIC FLOP CAME AT THE GRAMMYS IN early 2010, in her disastrous duet with Stevie Nicks. She sang "Rhiannon" with the rock & roll shawl queen, which should have been a proud pass-the-torch coronation moment. "It is a fairy tale and an honor to share a stage with Stevie Nicks," she announced. But she was off-key from her opening words, blowing note after note, enough to make a Welsh witch howl in pain. Her frantic dancing looked goofy next to Nicks, who just stood still and looked cool. Swift won four awards that night, including Album of the Year, but the commotion the next day was about her voice, questioning whether she could even carry a tune.

This was the first time many viewers heard her, outside the country markets, and many decided this kid was a tone-deaf amateur hype. Swift wasn't a real singer, which probably meant she wasn't a real anything else, and her Grammy was a joke. One typical reaction, from the *Washington Post*: "A night in the charmed life of Taylor Swift: Give an incredibly wretched vocal performance, go on to win the biggest Grammy of 2010 anyway." The *New York Times* called her "pitch-challenged." The backlash was so harsh, it inspired her to write "Mean."

The "Rhiannon" duet dogged her for years, hanging around her neck like a white-winged albatross. It's hardly unusual for singers to bomb at the Grammys—as Adele said a few years later, after the same kind of fiasco (mic malfunction, couldn't hear herself, out of tune), "Shit happens." But this was the moment when the world realized how fun it was to see Taylor fail. Even her biggest fans ate this up. Something about blondie just makes it great show-biz when she falls on her face. It's a consistent theme of her career, from "Rhiannon" to *Cats*, a movie people saw only as a chance to get high and laugh at her CGI fur. That's something about Taylor we learned early—when she fails, she doesn't do it modestly. Like Madonna, she's the kind of star whose flops are part of her legend.

Everything about Taylor punches people's buttons. Even her prolific work pace is insane. She's driven on a level that's just different from other artists. She's on a hot streak like Lil Wayne in 2007 or Bowie in 1977, one of those moments where an artist is cranking out brilliance faster than fans can keep up, except she's been riding that hot streak for nearly two decades. She never sits out a year, never pauses on new music, even while she's rerecording her entire catalog in her spare time. She's just tapped into some principle of frantic forward motion—like Lil Wayne said, real Gs move in silence like lasagna. But she's still young and peaking. Eighteen years in, even the greats tend to hit a dry spell. Let's put it this way: When David Bowie was at this point in his career, he was hitting the skids with his 1980s shoulder-pads era with *Never Let Me Down*. Prince was turning into the Artist Formerly Known As, with *Emancipation*. Springsteen was in his *Lucky Town* era. Dylan bottomed out in his preachy born-again phase. Stevie Wonder got lost in *The Secret Life of Plants*. (On the other hand, Madonna was on a roll with *Music*, and it's different if you count artists who started in groups.) These artists all had great albums ahead of them, so they weren't burned out—just hitting an edge-of-eighteen roadblock.

Taylor isn't there. She needs to be part of right now. We live in an age of larger-than-life pop icons, from Rihanna to Bad Bunny to Drake, from SZA to Harry Styles to Rosalía, but Taylor is always obsessed with being part of the moment. She arrived at a time when Beyoncé was setting new standards for how far pop could reach, as she's just kept going ever since. Bey could go years between albums, without losing any of her regal mystique, while refusing to speak a word in public. Taylor never had a prayer of emulating her reserve, but she came of age as Queen Bey was changing notions of what was possible. "I'm so glad I'll never know what my life would've been like without Beyoncé's influence," she wrote on Instagram in 2023, when they attended each other's concert-film premieres. "The way she's taught me and every artist out here to break rules and defy industry norms. Her generosity of spirit. Her resilience and versatility. She's been a guiding light throughout my career."

Taylor will always remain way too much. She's a compulsive overfeeler. She's never been a natural—all she does is try, try, try. In "Fifteen," she warned, "Don't forget to look before you fall," but like most of the wise, sensible advice she doles out, it's advice she's never considered following once in her life. Nobody loves taking leaps in the dark like our girl, the Queen of Never Looking Down. She's always had a zero-to-sixty heart, wired for melodramatic love and explosive flings and rude interruptions. There are many songs that tell this part of the Taylor story, but my favorite might be "Holy Ground" where she goes off the deep end about her intense soul connection with her latest crush, breathless about how much they have in common. Then she delivers the punch line: "And that was the first day!"

But when I hear these songs, I am not a visitor in someone else's life. She's written a couple hundred tunes that have a marvelous time ruining me, the songs for when I'm sliding into my feelings hard enough to snap a kneecap. Sometimes it feels like I'm hearing her read my diary aloud, making me feel garish and exposed. These songs have followed me through time as I've grieved and exulted and suffered. In my defense, I have none. There's something scary about all her try-try-try energy, but that's the only possible way she could write songs like these.

Taylor loves to lure people in to read her songs autobiographically while always keeping her deepest mysteries to herself. People love to speculate about Taylor the celebrity, Taylor the myth, Taylor the tabloid staple. That's the nature of the game, and that's part of the fun—I love playing that game as much as anyone does (though not as much as she does). But the most fascinating Taylor will always be the one in the music. She's the one none of us will ever understand—a jigsaw puzzle that turns out to be a mirror.

I LOVE YOU, IT'S RUINING MY LIFE

aylor once broke her songs down into three categories: Fountain Pen, Glitter Gel Pen, and Quill Pen. "I came up with these categories based on what writing tool I imagine having in my hand when I scribbled it down, figuratively," she said in 2022. "I don't actually have a quill. Anymore. I broke it once when I was mad."

The Fountain Pen songs are the most direct. "Most of my lyrics are 'Fountain Pen' lyrics," Swift said. "They're modern personal stories, written like poetry, about those moments you remember all too well where you can see, hear, and feel everything in screaming detail." The Quill songs are designed to "make you feel all old-fashioned, like you're a nineteenth-century poet crafting your next sonnet by candlelight." The Glitter Gel Pen is the party girl. "Glitter Gel Pen songs have lyrics that make you want to dance, sing, and toss glitter around the room," she said. "Glitter Gel Pen lyrics don't care if you don't take them seriously because they don't take themselves seriously. Glitter Gel Pen lyrics are the drunk girl at the party who tells you that you look like an angel in the bathroom."

Quill Pen Taylor is my favorite, the one who reigns on *Folklore* and *Evermore*. But she wouldn't be the same without the others. She needs to be jostled and irritated by Glitter Gel Pen. And they both need Fountain Pen. They're all so needy, elbowing each other for more of her attention as well as yours.

Taylor creates a narrator that many people feel like they know. When we talk about Taylor, sometimes it's the Taylor in the song, sometimes it's the real-life Taylor who wrote the song, sometimes there's confusion between them, and sometimes she's the one confused. It's like *The Divine Comedy*, where we have Dante Poet (the author) and Dante Pilgrim (the narrator). Taylor Songwriter may or may not be Taylor Pilgrim, Taylor Lover, Taylor Pathological People Pleaser, Taylor Mirrorball, or Taylor Hi I'm the Problem It's Me. She likes to keep cryptic about that. In a song like "Sweet Nothing," say, she's coy about the boundary between her and the narrator. (In real life, the couple broke up a few months later, so . . . no.) But she's right there in her songs.

Taylor has hit songs called "Shake It Off" and "You Need To Calm Down." She is utterly incapable of shaking it off, calming down, finding closure, skipping the conversation, forgetting you existed, or making a long story short. If she endorses one of these things in a song, you can bet your left lung she will break her own rule thirty seconds into the next song. Just like Paul McCartney, who sings "Let It Be" when he has never let anything be. Paul took thirty-two years to release his corrected "naked" remix of the Beatles' "Let It Be." I guarantee Taylor will still be rerecording "Shake

It Off" in 2046. She is relentlessly Taylor, flamboyantly and unreasonably and inadvisably and incessantly Taylor.

She holds on to her conviction that her moods are the universe and expressing them is why the universe exists. A great conviction for a songwriter, if more dubious for the rest of us. But whatever she's feeling, in any song, she throws herself in all the way. She sings about crying tears of mascara in a bathroom like it's an epic quest. She always overdoes it, never having one feeling when six would do. One of my favorite Tay lines, from "This Love": "I could go on and on, and I will." Yes, she will.

From a very young age, she was writing songs about her life and singing them in front of anybody who would listen. By "life" it's not meant to suggest that the lyrics have anything to do with any experiences she's lived out, just that everything is filtered through her sequestered perspective. She's always presented herself not just a witness but the author in her life story, turning all her worst experiences into songs. Yet she's always done it in a way that makes these experiences public property, to the point where she makes the world think of her as a character. She never considered *not* doing it this way, and there's no evidence to suggest any of the adults in her life advised her against it. Her liner notes for her first album: "To all the boys who thought they would be cool and break my heart, guess what? Here are 14 songs written about you. HA."

It's like Andy Warhol said in the Sixties, "If there's ever a problem, I film it and it's no longer a problem. It's a film."

ONE OF THE FIRST THINGS YOU DISCOVER IN THE TAY-lorverse: there are no accidents. She plans everything in advance.

She'll use the word "marvelous" in one song, "Starlight," about the Kennedys and fancy New England society, then file it away for years, waiting for the right moment, until slipping it into another song about fancy New England society, "The Last Great American Dynasty." An invisible string connecting two stories, two songs, two Taylors, that only the most obsessive fans are going to even notice. She'll sing about little kids playing pirates in two songs, eight years apart. In "The Best Day," she's with her doting mom and family, but in "Seven," from 2020, she's with a friend growing up in a miserable house, hiding in the closet from her angry dad. She wishes they could run away and be pirates, just beginning to understand her friend's pain. She's always playing the long game.

She's always had her eye on history, studying the songwriting greats and mastering their moves, tuned in to country and pop and soul and rock and Motown and the Brill Building and cheese-metal and new wave. She's a scholar of left-field music lore. "Jon Bon Jovi was the first rocker in the Eighties to smile a lot," she told *Rolling Stone*, at twenty-one. "I learned that on *Behind the Music* when I was, like, nine years old."

Her music is full of those strings, roaming through literature and history and film, to Emily Dickinson and Joni Mitchell and Jay-Z and Bob Dylan and Smokey Robinson and Shakespeare. She refuses to concede a thing to the idea that music is not designed to hold up to this kind of scrutiny. I'm fascinated by her bond with the poet Emily Dickinson. In 2024, the news broke that Swift and Dickinson are related—sixth cousins, three times removed. "If my lyrics sound like a letter written by Emily Dickinson's great-grandmother while sewing a lace curtain, that's me writing in the Quill genre," she said in 2022. She revealed her nineteenth-century-poetry fetish with "The Lakes," singing about Wordsworth and Coleridge, but clearly it wasn't a passing fancy. In her notes for *Midnights*, she signed off with the words "Keep the lanterns lit and go searching . . . We'll meet ourselves." The Emily Dickinson stan account @emilyorchard pointed out the connection to a letter that Dickinson wrote in 1855, telling a friend, "I am out with lanterns, looking for myself." (Later in the same letter, Dickinson writes, "I can't help laughing at my own catastrophe"—that sounds like that could come from a Swift song.) The Belle of Amherst has a late-night sensibility that they share, from "Good Morning—Midnight" to "Dreams—are well—but Waking's better" to "We grow accustomed to the Dark." It's the way her brain works. Everybody moved on. I stayed here.

Taylor and I have crossed paths a few times over the years, and I've been to her apartment to hear new albums, never while she was there. But I know her much better as a songwriter than I ever could as a person, and have an infinitely deeper connection with her music. When I say "Taylor" I'm talking about the Taylor who creates the music, and the Taylor she creates in the music. She's the one I actually know.

But when we've talked, we've mostly geeked out about music, and she's truly a geek's geek. Once when discussing the Beatles, she told me all about Alan Aldridge, the London artist who did their book *The Beatles Illustrated Lyrics* in 1969, appointed by John Lennon as "His Royal Master of Images to their Majesties the Beatles"—an obscure figure in Fabs folklore I'd never even heard of before. Taylor did a remarkable in-depth 2016 *Vogue* interview with Pattie Boyd, the muse for George Harrison and Eric Clapton, since Swift has drawn so much inspiration from her muses. When

I shared my arcane theory that "Getaway Car" is about the Pattie/ George/Eric love triangle, she immediately started combing her own song for more clues. You hear that in her work—Taylor is the world's biggest music nerd. But her geekdom is still a massively underrated aspect of her story, so it comes up plenty in this book.

She's also a generous laugher at terrible jokes. Tragically, I learned this one night backstage on the *1989* tour, after the U.S. Olympic Women's Soccer Team gave her an honorary team jersey. (Number thirteen, naturally.) I said, "You're wearing your new jersey—in New Jersey!" It was an Olympic-level athletic effort for her to force out a politely pained demi-laugh, to my undying shame, but I can say I have witnessed the sight of Taylor Swift being insincere, and it was downright heartwarming how bad she was at it.

I've been writing about her music since the get-go, but she never runs out of surprises. I keep a long-running list of her songs in *Rolling Stone*, ranking and reviewing every last one. The first time I compiled the list, after *1989*, she had 112 tunes, which already seemed like one of the all-time great songbooks. But she's up to nearly 300, more than doubling her life's work in the last decade. I'm constantly updating the list, moving songs up or down as they change for me over time, always cheating to keep "Fifteen" at fifteen. But two things never change: "All Too Well" at number one, "Bad Blood" at the bottom.

On opening night of the *Reputation* tour in 2018, in Glendale, Arizona, she warned me backstage she had a surprise. "I added 'All Too Well' to the set because of you," she said. "It's number one on your list. You changed my mind about that song. You convinced me it was more than just a Red Tour song." My trusty poker face must have failed me, because she looked concerned and asked, "Is it okay I told you this?" She sang a solo acoustic-guitar version that night—it was rare, I was there. But lest you get delusional about my influence, she immediately axed it from the set—that was just her wild-card spot—and played it only a handful of times for the rest of the tour. Meanwhile, she did "Bad Blood" every night. Just in case you've got her confused with somebody who listens to opinions.

In 2010, when I reviewed *Speak Now* in *Rolling Stone*, I wrote, "People like to fixate on Taylor Swift's youth, as if to say, yeah, she's pretty good for her age. But that just begs a question: Where are all the older people who are supposedly making better pop records than Taylor Swift? There aren't any." I compared her to Morrissey, my own personal teen idol of angst and melodrama. From a Smiths fanatic like me, the ultimate compliment. The Tay/Moz connections go deep—he sang, "The sun shines out of our behinds," she sang, "People throw rocks at things that shine," but they were coming from the same place. This review provoked angry mail from readers, including an aggrieved Morrissey fan who dismissed her as the "teenage nothing of the now." A wonderfully pithy phrase—I've always savored the rhythm of it. It sums up everything she was expected to be, given her age and her audience—that was her destined slot in the pop hierarchy. But that idea—that whole category—is just one of the clichés she set out to bulldoze.

A PORTRAIT OF THE ARTIST AS A YOUNG, LOUD, AND NOT-ESPECIALLY-GREAT-AT-CALMING-DOWN WOMAN

There are many people who are not fans of Taylor Swift, who for lack of a better collective noun I will designate "normal people." Some normal people seem to like her fine, for a song or two. Others don't. Many think she's nine-inch nails on a ten-mile chalkboard. These people have never had their lives ruined by a Taylor Swift song. You know what? They have chosen wisely. I envy them. They sleep soundly at night, not even wondering about whether "'Tis the Damn Season" happens in the same car as "Treacherous," or if "Dorothea" is about the heroine of *Middlemarch*.

Oh, the agonies and ecstasies of being a Taylor Swift fan. It's not like other fan experiences I've had. Why do I hear myself read so mercilessly in these songs? How the hell did a twenty-year-old write the hook "I feel you forget me like I used to feel you breathe"? Why does my friend in her forties text me to ask: "I just ugly cried on the way to goddamn Target. How can she write a song like 'Happiness'? It so perfectly captures what it feels like to be middle-aged and divorced. She's never been married she's in her 30s she's a witch a good witch but a witch"?

I've been a Taylor fan for a long time. But I'm not even close to figuring her out. I agonize over the details in these songs. I've spent an hour on the Q train each way just to hear "Coney Island" in Coney Island with the sun going down. ("Cornelia Street" sounds better in Coney Island, "Coney Island" sounds better on Cornelia Street.) I have wondered if the father who leaves in "Cardigan" is the careless man who leaves his careful daughter in "Mine," and if he's even the same father who sticks around and haunts his daughter's miserable childhood in "Seven." The traumatizing fathers on *Folklore* are a plotline in themselves.

Every Swiftie is full of stories. The stories about the song that changed their life, the song nobody appreciates the way they do, the song they listened to on their fifteenth birthday. Fans love their stories as much as they love the songs. Sometimes I even wonder if we keep going back to the songs because we just want to create more of the stories. But it's more like this: we go to these songs because they tell us *our* stories. We tell our secrets to these songs, and they scream our secrets back at us. We bring our questions to these songs, the way Taylor asks the streetlights, "Will it be okay?" And the streetlights give her the exact same answer that Stevie Nicks got from the mirror in the sky, all those years ago: "I don't know."

Taylor fans also love to argue. We'll argue about every last detail in the lyrics—we can argue forever about what the lyrics even are. She tries to settle the arguments—it's "a long list of ex-lovers," not "Starbucks lovers"—but we still insist on hearing the songs our own way. To me, it's always "the lights and boys are blinding" in "New Romantics," not "lights and noise," yet I can't justify this empirically. Do you hear "grinning like a devil" or "pretty little devil"? "I spent forever" or "I spin forever"? "The Archer" always sounds like she's singing "I've got a hundred donuts and peaches." If you're a fan of the great Nineties indie rock band Slint, you probably hear "Bejeweled" as "I miss you, but I miss *Spiderland*."

Taylor has these kinds of fans because she's terrible at settling arguments—what she's really into is starting new ones. She has kept trying on different musical and emotional identities all through her career. She leaves her Old Taylors behind, but she never really gives up on any of them, so she just keeps collecting New Taylors. Country Taylor, Goth Taylor, Pop Glitz Taylor—she takes them all along with her, which is why listening to her albums often feels like eavesdropping on them while they argue. They're all a little needier than they want to be. They get jealous of each other. They all have boundary issues, none of them are great at reading the room, yet I'm grateful for every one of them. But she keeps burning through these New Taylors without losing any of her essential weirdness, which (fortunately) she's stuck with. But all these different Taylors sound like the real thing, because they're all part of the same difficult-but-real woman. As she said in 2022, her music includes,

"My friends and my fiercest fans and my harshest detractors and everyone who entered my life or left it. Because when it comes to my songwriting and my life, they are one in the same. As the great Nora Ephron once said, 'Everything is copy.'"

Sometimes Taylor loves to brag about her self-awareness, in ways that make you wonder if she's ever met herself. In "You're on Your Own Kid," she sings, "I play it cool with the best of them." *Riiiiight*—this is the same Taylor who sang "Delicate," where she boasts about how chill and cool and secure she is, then elbows you in the ribs to ask "Isn't it? Isn't it?" until she feels sure that you notice. There are twenty-six "isn't it"s in that song and, tragically, I hear myself in every single one of them. Sometimes she tries to come off as a relatable and ordinary narrator, yet that just makes her sound more like she's in a world of her own. (A handwritten sign I spotted taped to a door backstage on the *1989* tour: "Cats Roaming. Do Not Open." Only on Planet Taylor.) As she describes herself accurately in "Hits Different," she's always going to be that Argumentative Antithetical Dream Girl.

But when I hear myself in her songs, it's often the parts of me I try hardest to keep covered up and tied down. I'm threatened by the hairpin trigger in her songs, her constant edge of emotional danger. She likes her slopes treacherous and her paths reckless. I'm wired the opposite way—on the spectrum of Careless Man and Careful Daughter, I skew extremely Careful D. I'm not a fan of impulsive, awkward blurts that can't be walked back. I avoid scenes. I'm totally cool with not knowing if the high was worth the pain. But if you go to pop songs looking for tidy resolutions, you're not going to get much out of Taylor. She's not big on letting go and moving on. She doesn't ever stick to writing one song at a time—she plants seeds for future songs. That's why you can listen to these songs for years and then get ambushed by one you never noticed. For years I thought "You Are In Love" was a sweet little novelty, maybe a bit far on her whimsical side for me, but not my personal cup. But now every second of it gets me, right from the synth intro, before she even opens her mouth. That whole vocal. The way she sings "sidewalks," damn. Or "shoulders." "For once." "Downtown." "Best friend."

"Long Live" is her most giant-hearted rock anthem—her "Born to Run," her "Common People," her "We Are the Champions." She gets to the ending, *then* swerves into a whole new song and changes the topic to *making him promise to stand by her forever*. Oh, Taylor, what a mess. How can this poor guy live up to that promise? "So, kids, gather around. This picture is Auntie Taylor. Yeah, the one who posts on your Instagram to say, 'Hope it's nice where you are.' The one who sends the holiday card every year that says, 'I'm sure that you got a wife and kids out there. Merry Christmas.' Well, this is her. She hopes you shine. Don't tell your mom we had this conversation, okay? Your mom is actually not a huge fan of Auntie Taylor.") Couldn't she save this for the next song?

But Taylor is incapable of saving anything for the next song. That "leaving like a father" line in "Cardigan" sneaks up at the end—it's almost finished, then she drops that "leaving like a father" and moves on. She makes it sound like someone putting their all, every feeling, every love, every hate, into the one song they have in them, like this song has to contain all the other stories they won't get to tell. This is my first song, my last song, she seems to say. I'm not holding back a thing for any next song. This is *it*.

The day she wrote this song with the National's Aaron Dessner, she posted a photo with the caption "Not a lot going on at the moment." Why do we ever believe a damn word she says?

4

EARLY DAYS: PLEASE PICTURE ME IN THE TREES

There's a moment in the Eras Tour when Taylor changes outfits offstage. Her voice speaks, in a collage of her lyrics: "If you wish to romanticize the woman I became, then say you'll remember me. Standing in a nice dress. Staring at the sunset. Or you could begin at the beginning."

So: the beginning. She was born in Pennsylvania on December 13, 1989. The number one song at the time was Billy Joel's "We Didn't Start the Fire." She grew up on a fifteen-acre Christmas tree farm, with her father, Scott; her mother, Andrea; her younger brother, Austin; and seven horses. Her parents had careers in finance: Scott was an investment banker turned vice president at Merrill Lynch; Andrea had been a marketing executive, and she figured her daughter would follow in her parents' corporate footsteps. "She wanted me to be a businessperson in a business world," she told *Rolling Stone*. Her parents might have named her after James Taylor, but they also thought an androgynous name would help in a male-dominated business world: "She named me Taylor so that if anybody saw on a business card the name Taylor, they wouldn't know if it was a girl or a guy if they were thinking of hiring me."

Her parents got married in 1988—in a random coincidence of pop history, the same day that Rihanna was born. They moved out to the country, an hour outside Philly, so the kids could have a rural childhood. Young Taylor was a horse girl, riding in competitions, and then a theater kid. She played plum roles in her local theater academy: Maria in *The Sound of Music*, Sandy in *Grease*, Kim in *Bye Bye Birdie*. All leads—you can guess how the other kids (and their parents) appreciated that, so maybe it's no surprise the academy went out of business.

She found her vocation when she heard LeAnn Rimes's debut *Blue*, a gift for her sixth birthday. She became an obsessive country fan. "I started listening to female country artists nonstop: Faith Hill, Shania Twain, Dixie Chicks," she said in 2007. "And they led me back to Patsy Cline and Loretta Lynn and Tammy Wynette. I think it was the storytelling that really grabbed me."

Andrea and Scott weren't stage parents—they didn't know diddly about showbiz, weren't into country music. Neither would have picked this career path, but they knew drive when they saw it. Taylor and Andrea began traveling to New York for voice lessons and Broadway auditions. Through some string-pulling, she sang the national anthem at a 2002 76ers playoff game, with Jay-Z sitting courtside. (He high-fived her and said, "Beautiful.") She sang "America the Beautiful" at the US Open. She kept crashing talent shows and karaoke contests; she showed up at one bar for a weekly open-mic competition for eighteen months until she won. The big prize: she got to open for Charlie Daniels, even if it was an all-day festival where she went on at 10:30 a.m.

None of this played with her peers. Old folks thought this precocious child was charming; young folks thought she was a drag. Country was not cool at her school, where steel guitars and Southern drawls were déclassé signifiers. By her own account, Taylor was a laughingstock in middle school, with her talent shows and blue ribbons and—get this—Christmas trees. "I guess I'm just not good enough for people my own age," she wrote in her eighth-grade diary. "Or maybe I'm not bad enough?" She spent her school days making enemies, which proved to be a lifelong skill. But intriguingly, when she dropped her debut, she made a documentary called *A Place in This World*, which focused on how tight she was with her high school circle of friends, seen singing along with her. Many of the kids speak on camera about how popular she is. She dropped that narrative almost immediately.

So it's an open question. Was she authentically shy in high school, where she spent just one year? Did she really go through the tribulations of adolescent rejection? But does it really matter? Bruce Springsteen didn't even know how to drive when he wrote "Thunder Road." Tupac was a ballet dancer and drama student in high school, not a gangster. Brian Wilson couldn't surf. But she's always mythologized her high-school outcast days. She was still in her teens when she told *Glamour*, "I remember seeing girls crying in the bathroom every Monday about what they did at a party that weekend. I never wanted to be that girl." It's ironic because Taylor invented crying in the bathroom—nobody has shed more tears in more facilities since indoor plumbing was invented. She owns the concept, whether or not she's done it in real life. Vowing not to be that girl was a guarantee she'd go on to epitomize that girl.

Her best friend was Abigail Anderson, who became the heroine of "Fifteen." (They stayed together for life; Taylor was recently a bridesmaid at her wedding.) As Abigail recalled, "We were the ones in the back of the class saying negative things about *Romeo and Juliet* because we were so bitter toward that emotion at the time."

Taylor recorded a demo at eleven, singing along with a karaoke machine. She had that Southern twang in her voice—not an accent she was raised with, but that was just what country singers did. She did her best Dolly Parton ("Here You Come Again"), LeAnn Rimes ("One Way Ticket"), the Dixie Chicks ("There's Your Trouble"), and Olivia Newton-John, for "Hopelessly Devoted to You." Her mom drove her to Nashville, so Taylor could cruise Music Row and drop off her demo. Taylor walked in cold to twenty different record labels, leaving her CD at twenty different front desks, as the receptionists found polite ways to say, "You are one brave but delusional and slightly scary eleven-year-old." Andrea never came in—she walked Taylor to the front door, then waited in the car. This girl was going to have to make her own sales pitch. On each demo CD, Taylor wrote, "Call me!"

When nobody called, she figured she wasn't working hard enough. Taylor started playing guitar; the first song she learned was Cheap Trick's "I Want You to Want Me." She wrote a song of her own just a few hours later—"Lucky You," she called it. "There's a little girl in this little town," Taylor was singing. "With a little too much heart to go around." The guitar gave her a feeling of mysterious power. "For the first time, I could sit in class and those girls could say anything they wanted about me, because after school I was going to go home and write a song about it."

Her little town was about to get bigger. When she was thirteen, her parents moved the family to Nashville. She got a few meetings, playing her tunes, and moved fast. She signed her first publishing deal at fourteen and a development deal with RCA. There was sneering in Nashville about this dilettante brat whose rich parents were buying her a music career. When her RCA deal was up, they offered another year, but she didn't want to keep waiting to get in the studio. "I don't want to be an adult country singer. I want to get out there as soon as possible," she said at the time. "A young pop singer is fourteen years old. A young country singer is twenty-nine years old."

She got a break when Maybelline put her song "The Outside" on a CD they gave to customers, *Chicks with Attitude*. Maybelline also sponsored a Chicks with Attitude tour, featuring Liz Phair and the Cardigans, though she wasn't invited. (What a shame: imagine Liz and Taylor teaming up for a duet on "Divorce Song.") She also appeared in an Abercrombie & Fitch "Rising Stars" ad campaign, as well as the A & F catalog. She posed for a hilariously corny photo where she stands there crying, wiping away tears with one hand, holding her guitar in the other. The photo ran in *Vanity Fair*, with another dozen Rising Stars, but she's easily the goofiest photo in the bunch; the others nuzzle horses or play with their hair. Michelle Trachtenberg (already famous on *Buffy the Vampire Slayer*) sits in a tree swing. It's hard to see without snickering now—not the image she wanted to project. But that's the first Taylor to appear in print: the quintessential Sad Girl, half teardrops, half guitar.

She played the prestigious Bluebird Cafe, where Scott Borchetta first heard her sing. He was a Nashville PR guy starting a new label with the not-quite-a-joke name Big Machine Records. (He took it from a Velvet Revolver album.) Taylor's dad invested in the label, a 3 percent stake. It was the first time she'd been on a team, or at least one that didn't involve girls throwing basketballs at her head. "Scott Borchetta, thank you for believing in me since I was 14," she wrote in the *Fearless* notes, "and still trying to straighten my hair." She added, "You're family."

The label had ideas about producers. She had one idea: Nathan Chapman, whom she'd met cutting demos. Not a name producer— he'd never even produced an album, let alone a hit. Fresh out of college, he wasn't much more experienced than she was. She got her way. *Taylor Swift* came out in October 2006. Her coded meaning for the song "Cold as You" was "time to let go." It wasn't the last time she'd give herself that advice.

Please picture her at fifteen, making her way in the music biz, when most people figured she had hit her peak just by releasing an album. She was already romanticizing the woman she would become. Too scared to jump in? Least of her problems.

5

TRACK FIVE: THE BALLAD
OF "ALL TOO WELL"

13.

October 2012: Taylor Swift releases her greatest song, "All Too
Well." It's the heart of *Red*, a gigantic rock & roll power ballad. It
builds from a hushed girl-at-her-piano confession to her loudest,
most passionate vocal thunder. She begins with a lost scarf, left at
her ex-boyfriend's sister's house, but she blows up that trivial detail
into a heartbreak epic. "All Too Well" peaks about six times, then
calms down . . . then she tears up her masterpiece and starts the
song over. If you've got five minutes to persuade a jury to convict
her of being one of the all-time greats as a singer, songwriter, tortured poet, oversharer, bridge crafter, chorus yeller, the works, it's
the one you play.

"All Too Well" isn't a hit—not even a single. Definitely not one
you'd hear on the radio. Just a deep cut cherished by her most ar-
dent fans. After the Red Tour, she won't sing it live again for years.
This song is strictly for the hardcore, a note passed in secrecy from
fan to fan, kept as an oath. If it's your song, that means you're in

the inner circle—probably a hopeless case. You can't get rid of it, because you remember it.

November 2021: Taylor releases "All Too Well (10 Minute Version)," from her new *Red (Taylor's Version)*. She makes it twice as long and twice as intense, adding the long-lost verses she cut from her early drafts. Yet this is the version that turns into a number one hit—the first ten-minute chart-topper ever in *Billboard*. It's nobody's secret now—it belongs to the world. The strange journey of "All Too Well" is one of my favorite music stories ever. Hers too, probably.

12.

Taylor has a mystique about her Track Fives. On any given album, it's the emotional bloodbath. "All Too Well" is the most famous of all Track Fives, but they never fail. "My Tears Ricochet" on *Folklore*. "White Horse" on *Fearless*. "Delicate" on *Reputation*. "The Archer" on *Lover*. "Tolerate It" on *Evermore*. "Dear John" on *Speak Now*. "So Long, London" on *The Tortured Poets Department*. "You're on Your Own, Kid" on *Midnights*. ("Cold as You" on the debut passes the test, but not the bouncy "All You Had to Do Was Stay" on *1989*, which feels more like a track nine.)

11.

My "All Too Well" obsession has grown since it first dropped on *Red*. I've kept listening, writing about it, butchering it at karaoke. It goes where I go. When she first announced she was unleashing the long-rumored ten-minute version, I hoped it might add a cool footnote to my favorite song. But now it's just the song. It destroys crowds every night on the Eras Tour. It set a new record as the longest number one hit in history, dethroning "American Pie." (The courtroom was adjourned; the scarf was not returned.) But it only exists because fans called her bluff—after she mentioned the original draft, people kept asking about it, as if she had it hidden in a sock drawer. She must have wished many times that she'd kept her mouth shut. But all this talk inspired her to go back and open up a story she thought was finished. Just imagine, these extra verses were sitting there for years gathering dust, just waiting for their time.

Next, Taylor directed a short film of the song. When I saw her premiere the film in a New York City theater, in front of a few hundred fans, she sang the new version solo, on her acoustic guitar. She introduced it with a few words, thanking her fans for rescuing it from oblivion. "A record label didn't pick this as a single. It was my favorite," she said. "It was about something very personal to me. It was very hard to perform it live. Now for me, honestly, this song is one hundred percent about us and for you."

Every version of "All Too Well" tells a different story. The original five-minute *Red* version, which has never lost any of its power. The ten-minute epic, looking back in anger. There's the "Sad Girl Autumn Version" from the Long Pond Studio sessions, with Aaron Dessner on piano. That acoustic solo performance. The Eras Tour stadium sing-along. But each version feels like it's all her, because this isn't really a song about a boy—never was. It's about a girl, her piano, her memory, and her refusal to surrender her most painful secrets, even when it's tempting to forget.

10.

"I really do write about girlhood a lot," Taylor said in 2022, at the Tribeca Film Festival. "I'm very fascinated and always have been with this phase of becoming a young woman where you're this very fragile and vulnerable age. I think nineteen and twenty is such a profound age for young women." For her, at the age of thirty-three, that's the story she sees when she looks back at "All Too Well." "I think there's a moment when you're nineteen or twenty where your heart is so susceptible to just getting broken, getting shattered, and your sense of self goes out the window so quickly, and it's such a formative age. I wanted to tell that story, about girlhood calcifying into this bruised adulthood."

9.

February 2014: a miserable gray Saturday afternoon. I'm walking around Brooklyn, in heavy snow, feeling dismal and defeated. Someone I love is in trouble, digging themselves deeper. I'm just making it worse when I try to help. I keep listening to two songs on my iPod: "All Too Well" and "Dear John." They're the only songs that feel clumsy and glum and wintry enough to fit my mood. The pain in them is physically cumbersome—they lumber from verse to verse, carrying too many burdens to walk straight. Both songs with a payoff at the end: she's so weary from the solitary burden of memory, she decides to stop lugging it. In the final line of "Dear John," she switches from "I should have known" to "YOU should have known." In "All Too Well," she goes from "I remember it all" to "YOU remember it all." The feminist rage is there in her voice, as she recalls a certain trauma, unsure if she will be believed or even taken seriously. Her older self checks in on her barely younger self and insists that she really saw what she saw and she really felt what she felt and it all really happened.

It conjures up a teenage flashback, hearing Madonna on the radio, singing "Live to Tell," another long, somber pop ballad, built for sad winter days. Another young girl with a story she's been told not to remember. Both hits sound shiny and bright on the surface. Hearing them in the wild, in bus stations or pizzerias, you might wonder: *Are all these people hearing it? Do they notice?* Taylor is a true daughter of Madonna—she needs to connect on that pop pleasure level, whatever moods she's expressing, so these songs are designed to work even if you're in a summer mood. But today, they belong deep in the snow.

8.

Right from the start, as soon as "All Too Well" came out, she loved to tell the story of how she wrote it. "It would be kind of weird to finish a song and be like, 'And this moment, I shall remember,'" Taylor told *Rolling Stone* years later. "'This guitar hath been anointed with my sacred tuneage!'"

The song originated at a sound check, when she began strumming those chords, going off on a freestyle about her recent breakups. As she recalled, "My band joined in and I went on a rant." She wanted to hang on to this idea. "I called my friend and cowriter Liz Rose and I said, 'Come over, we've gotta filter this down.' It took me a really long time to get it to its final form." Rose was her songwriting sensei, a Music Row vet who mentored Taylor when she came to town, showing her the ropes and playing a major role on her early records. "Basically, I was her editor," Rose said in 2008. "She'd write about what happened in school that day. She had such a clear vision of what she wanted to say. And she's come in with the most incredible hooks." Until Taylor, Rose's biggest successes were Gary Allan's hit "Songs About Rain"—obviously she and Taylor were destined to meet—and a Tim McGraw album cut.

When she talked about "All Too Well" in the early days, she told this story, sometimes verbatim. It looked like a smokescreen—it was easier to roll out the canned origin story than talk about the actual song. "'All Too Well' was the hardest to write," she said on *Good Morning America*, when asked by a fan named TheLuckyOne1313. "It started out being probably like a ten-minute song, which you can't put on an album. And I had to filter it down to a story that could work in the form of a song."

But it was tantalizing to hear about that ten-minute version. Where was it? When would we hear the director's cut? She wasn't bluffing, was she? "I'm promoting so many albums, went on so many tours, tried to move past the *Red* album," she said in 2022. "And every time I would talk to you—every time I'm doing a livestream, every time there's a Q & A, every time there's a meet-and-greet, there's 'When are you going to release the ten-minute version of 'All Too Well?' You guys just wouldn't let it go."

7.

The "All Too Well" short film begins with an epigraph from the Chilean poet Pablo Neruda, one she has relied upon before, having quoted it in the prologue of *Red* in 2012. "There's an old poem by Neruda that I've always been captivated by, and one of the lines in it has stuck with me ever since the first time I read it. It says, 'Love is so short, forgetting is so long.' It's a line I've related to in my saddest moments, when I needed to know someone else had felt that exact same way."

6.

The fact that it wasn't a hit added to the original mystique—a buried treasure, too Taylor for prime time. She sang it at the Grammys in 2013, solo at her piano. She did her triple-axel hair-whipping and head-banging, a shameless rock-star stunt—you'd have to go back to a Temple of the Dog or Tori Amos video to see such acrobatic hair windmills. But it was an eccentric pick for her spotlight, facing her biggest global TV audience with a song hardly anyone knew. She didn't touch her crowd-pleasing *Red* hits. It didn't seem to make sense.

5.

The legend of the ten-minute draft kept building, until she went back to complete it—by then, the song was in charge, and the writer was merely taking orders. She released it on *Red (Taylor's Version)* in November 2021. She adds extra verses about this guy tossing his key chain and meeting her dad and her twenty-first birthday party. When her boyfriend doesn't show up at midnight, her dad tries to cheer her up—the first time he's quoted in a song. He tells her, "It's supposed to be fun, turning twenty-one." She cries while bystanders ask her what happened. ("You! That's what happened! You!") She sharpens her adult anger, looking back at the power dynamics of a relationship with an older man. She hits harder about the age difference, jeering, "I'll get older, but your lovers stay my age."

She sang about this birthday in "The Moment I Knew," in 2012, and years later in "Happiness," on *Evermore*, recalling "the dress I wore at midnight." ("Happiness" came out on the eve of her thirty-first birthday—ten years after the party.) At the end of "The Moment I Knew," the boy calls to tell her he's sorry. She says, "I'm sorry, too," then catches herself saying it. That was the moment she knew. Not the last time she'd apologize to a man for what he did, then spend years wondering why.

4.

In the Swiftian universe, any lost scarf is a ticking time bomb that can take years to explode into a song. No scrap of the past is safe from showing up again—no snow globe, no snowmobile, no snow or beach. She's a detective who never files the cold cases away.

As another great poet of teen angst, Steven Patrick Morrissey, would say: there is a refrigerator light that never goes out.

3.

November 2021: Taylor premieres her fifteen-minute short film in New York, the day the album drops. A thirteen-plex on the Upper West Side. They hand out "All Too Well" pocket-tissue packs at the door. (Not souvenirs, either—they get audibly used.) A loud crowd, a fun crowd, gasping with pain when Sadie Sink curls up on her bed, heckling Dylan O'Brien. The rad Swiftie next to me who flew up from North Carolina (a "Mirrorball" gal) yells, "Fuck you, Jake!" There were cheers for the close-up of her red typewriter.

I see it on the big screen, eight months later, in a different atmosphere: the Tribeca Film Festival. It's a rare public appearance for Taylor—she hasn't been spotted anywhere all year. A sizable portion of the audience doesn't know or care much about her—they're here for the festival, older, maler, accompanied by the Swifties in their lives. (You can tell who's who when the festival director says she's "enchanted" to have Swift there.) On the way into the theater, the ticket person tells me, "Have a marvelous time"—so maybe everybody is an honorary Swiftie today. But it's definitely the first time I've ever seen her walk on to polite applause. She knows she's on foreign turf, and she's eager to impress. It's so surreal to see her work to win people over.

She pivots to Film Geek (Taylor's Version), in a Q & A with indie director Mike Mills. "I love this John Cassavetes quote," she says early on, "where he says, 'I've never seen an exploding helicopter. I've never seen anybody go and blow somebody's head off. So why should I make films about them? But I *have* seen people destroy themselves in the smallest way.' Whoa—I *felt* that."

She discusses that Neruda epigraph, calling it "a line that haunted me and still haunts me. It's a violent thing to read something that poignant." The great Chilean poet was a worldwide legend in his own time—but even he probably never imagined that future teenagers would scream at the sight of his name. I'm randomly sitting next to one of my heroes, the great director Jim Jarmusch, who was talking about how he'd never heard her before, but he's laughing now, charmed by her self-effacing jokes. When Mike Mills praises her narrative flair, saying, "You're really good at . . . ," she chimes in with "Drama?" Mills spends the Q & A asking about her nuts-and-bolts creative process—I've never heard her do an interview this nerdy. The most surprising revelation: the ending of "All Too Well" is based on the Old Hollywood grande dame Barbara Stanwyck in *Stella Dallas*, the 1937 King Vidor drama. That scene of the ex-boyfriend standing outside in the cold, wearing her old scarf?

She stole that from the final scene, where Stanwyck watches her estranged daughter's wedding, as she marries into New York high society. She isn't invited, so she stands on the sidewalk, peering through the window. That's how the "All Too Well" film ends—but as far as I can find online, nobody caught that reference.

I became a big Stanwyck fan in my early thirties, weeping over her movies late at night, alone on my couch, watching her suffer in style. It makes sense Swift is a fan. Nobody had presence like Barbara Stanwyck—*The Lady Eve* is her "Cowboy Like Me" (a con artist loves the game too much to fall in love with a mark), *Forty Guns* her "Last Great American Dynasty" (rich lady with a mean streak). My personal fave is one nobody else likes, *My Reputation*, a soapy melodrama from 1946. She's a young war widow who becomes the shame of her small town. The best scene: she looks around her living room, once a respectable married home, now a den of sin, and sighs, "Women on the loose can be such a mess."

2.

Did you know Stevie Nicks lost a velvet jacket once? A quintessential Seventies rock story. Cameron Crowe wrote a news bulletin for *Rolling Stone*, in the Stevie-crazed summer of 1978. Not just any velvet jacket—her extra-special magic lucky jacket, the antique black velvet jacket she wore onstage every night when it was time for "Landslide." She lost it in LA (where else) at a Warren Zevon show (really, where else). "Nicks has all but given up on it being returned," *Rolling Stone* reports. "Facing the upcoming Fleetwood Mac tour without the jacket, she says, 'It's irreplaceable and means a whole lot more to me than to whomever took it.' Any information would be appreciated." There's a hotline number. The photo depicts her in black mourning clothes, with a widow's veil.

I like to imagine this jacket is still out there, in the great cosmic rock & roll lost-and-found bin, snuggled up with Taylor's scarf. The lost girls of rock & roll, they remember the sacred relics that get left behind. Nobody else will ever fucking understand.

1.

Taylor comes back to these "All Too Well" piano chords sometimes, when she's telling a sad story, like "Cornelia Street" or "Champagne Problems." She spends these songs looking into her future, wondering how her older self will feel about her turmoil now. But her stories keep on telling themselves, long after she's finished writing the song. "All Too Well" keeps evolving, expanding, beyond anything she could have imagined. It's a song to get passed around until it comes back as something new. Maybe this thing was always going to be a masterpiece. But it can't turn into a masterpiece until she tears it all up.

THE FANGIRL

An eternal law of pop music: anything halfway cool that's ever happened is because teenage girls made it happen. Everybody knows they're the fans who can't be fooled. They're the fans who never lie. They have zero incentive to fake it. This is why everyone else in the music biz is terrified of teenage girls. Everyone else can be cajoled, conned, taken for granted. Teenage girls can't. History is littered with the charred remains of pop stars who've played fickle with them, trying to upgrade to more respectable adult audiences. History shows the girls are not slow to punish this. When you ditch the girls to impress other audiences, you impress nobody. A friend to all is a friend to none; chase two girls, lose the One.

Taylor knows who the One is. She started out as a teenage girl singing directly to her peers, and even as she conquered the world, she never lost those girls, because she's never stopped putting them first, even as they keep growing up into their thirties, forties, fifties. She loves girls who love music, and she changed the world to make room for them.

Phoebe Bridgers was one of the archetypal teen fans listening in. "I had big feelings and I wanted to write songs about them," she said in 2022. "But songs were written by adults about their very adult lives. So, when I started writing, I just made stuff up, and the songs sucked. I knew that, and I fantasized about the day far in the future when I'd finally have something to say when I'd lived a life worth writing a song about."

That fantasy changed when she heard Swift, listening to country radio with her mom. "I heard a girl not much older than me singing a song she had written about her own life, and the song was really good. As I grew up, so did Taylor and so did her songs. Gradually my songs started to suck less because instead of trying to sound interesting, I just started telling the truth. Taylor has always told the truth." The world was a different place now. "I'm grateful to have grown up in a world with Taylor Swift in it," Bridgers said. "Or, *The World: Taylor's Version*."

"WOMEN MAKE SHOW BUSINESS," SMOKEY ROBINSON TOLD *Rolling Stone* in 1979. "Men contribute to the thing, but women actually make show business happen. Men can sit and watch [pop-jazz singer] Nancy Wilson all night long and never go, 'Oooooooh,' but women—if they feel like screaming, they do it." Paul McCartney knew the secret, right at the dawn of Beatlemania. "At the time we were eighteen, nineteen, whatever," he told Beatles scholar Mark Lewisohn in 1987, "so you're talking to all girls who are seventeen. We were quite conscious of that. We wrote for our market. We knew if we wrote a song called 'Thank You Girl' that a lot of the girls who wrote us fan letters would take it as a genuine thank-you."

But Taylor's connection to her girl fans goes deeper—she started as one of them, and she's managed to grow with them. It all begins with one question: "LeAnn, did you get my letters?"

Taylor went to see her first idol LeAnn Rimes live, at the age of eight. "I was holding up this huge banner in the front row," she recalled around the time of her debut. "It's like 'I love you, LeAnn' like a stalker, and I had sent her all these letters and this package of drawings and pictures of me and stuff to her hotel room the night before." So far, so Taylor. "I had a HUGE blond 'fro when I was little, like it's a lot bigger than it is now," Swift said. "So she recognized me in the audience. And had actually taken time to read my letters and stuff." After the show, Taylor pressed in close. "When she was going around shaking hands with people in the audience she looked down and I was like, 'LeAnn, did you get my letters?' And she goes, 'I sure did, Taylor.'"

LeAnn Rimes created a goddamn monster. She warped this child into being the best to *ever* do what LeAnn did. For Taylor, that was the primal scene of instruction. "That was it," she recalled. "That was the moment where literally it all just clicked for me." That moment of LeAnn Rimes remembering Taylor's name had a massive impact on the world we live in now—it formed Taylor's idea of how a pop star rolls, raising the standard so high that it's now just part of any rookie pop star's job. We owe LeAnn so much.

Taylor's stamina for romancing the fans was off the charts from the start. She thrives on that energy. In her prepandemic tours, she did hours of fan meet-and-greets before every show, then hours of them afterward. She works the room in a way that might be more like political candidates than other singers. A political journalist told me the only person he'd seen with that specific charisma was

Bill Clinton. She turns on the crowd because she gets turned on by the crowd and the fans because she's one of them.

She was absurdly kind to my nieces in 2013, in Nashville, having no clue who they were or how they got here. They road-tripped from Atlanta for the last stand of the *Red* tour. Five tween girls, two moms, the girls with red glitter all over their faces, in homemade outfits with T-shirts saying, "You can't spell HERO without HER." The girls shivered in a corner backstage, waiting in case they got a moment, but broke the ice when they started recognizing her band members. This made them popular, since they knew their names and which songs they played on. "This never happens to us," her bassist told my sister. The girls cried buckets (the moms said, "Crying is okay, screaming is not") as the red glitter on their faces melted into gunk. Andrea Swift took a shine to them and gave them pit passes. Scott Swift gave them guitar picks.

Taylor Swift walked by on her way to the stage. She was already dressed to go out and sing "State of Grace," in her white shirt and black hat. But she saw five random girls. Quite honestly, she should not have been allowed anywhere near sobbing children, least of all weepy girls with sticky wet red goop all over their faces. She was wearing her stage shirt, no time to change. She hugged them all. My niece, only eight, sobbed, "I've been listening to you since I was three!"

Taylor said, "Well, honey, I guess that means we grew up together."

Then she was whisked up the stairs to the stage, still in that white shirt, not a single goop stain, to face her hometown crowd. Was this line just part of her standard canned banter? I've asked around, yet that doesn't seem to be the case. (She said it years later in the *Miss Americana* doc.) The girls called me after the show, while out for breakfast at midnight, still crying too hard to talk. I was more shocked than they were. There's so much in this story I've never wrapped my head around—what were her handlers thinking? What was *she* thinking? It's just one of the mysteries she's left in her wake. But it might give a clue to the mystery that this artist and these fans have built together.

FEARLESS

The first time I heard *Fearless* was over the phone. The label was so paranoid about leaks, they didn't even want to play it for me in a private room in case I was wearing a wire. I had high hopes, but I couldn't believe how great this one was. *Holy cats*, I thought. *This is a perfect pop record. One of the all-time perfect pop records. A classic. She'll never top it.* Then she topped it with her next album, and the one after that, and topped it so many times that *Fearless* became overshadowed for a while. She gave it a place of honor in the *Taylor's Version* series by remaking this one first.

Fearless introduced Taylor Swift as we know her—it created the image that made her a star, the image she's reacted against in so many ways since. It was her world-building album, with all her favorite tropes: cars; windows; pebbles; dresses; rain, so much rain, buckets of rain; photo albums; tears; doorways. It sets out the Taylor personality—the teen country songwriter, always falling in love, bedeviled by the boyfolk, making the thrills and spills of a week-long high school romance sound as torchy as one of Patsy Cline's marriages. A girl who applies her mascara with great care because she plans to cry it all off. A girl who wears her best dress to go ride around in a storm. She likes to make a scene. In "Forever & Always," when she sings, "It rains in your bedroom"—a very in-character Taylor predicament.

She wrote or cowrote all the songs, rare then for either country singers or teenage pop divas. *Fearless* has an old-school side one/ side two divide, and she was already savvy enough to front-load the bangers. It begins with a monster six-song run: "Fearless," "Fifteen," "Love Story," "Hey Stephen," "White Horse," "You Belong with Me." She saves the weepy piano longueurs for the flip side, having learned the art of album pacing, with "Hey Stephen" as a light sorbet to cleanse the palate, in between so many heavy courses. It's easy to overlook, compared to its neighbors, but it's a clever nod to the girl-group tradition, with the Ronettes' "Be My Baby" beat. It's also got the first memorable "Taylor laughs at her own joke" moment, when she chuckles, "All those other girls, well, they're beautiful / But would they write a song for you?" "Love Story" was her version of *Romeo and Juliet*, coming back stronger than a 1590s trend.

Fearless also gave her the image of the girl who sang about her exes. There's a classic moment a few years later, on the red carpet at the Golden Globes, where she's chatting with Ryan Seacrest. He shows her a clip from this era, on his radio show, roasting one of her boyfriends. She laughs, with not-quite-embarrassed amusement, and says, "Yeah, I was a little mouthy when I was eighteen." Yes, Taylor, you sure were, which is how songs like this happen. It helped that Joe Jonas was her most famous ex so far, but also that he gave her the juiciest breakup anecdote, dumping her over the phone in twenty-nine seconds. He soon followed with the first notable anti-Taylor answer song, on the JoBros' *Lines, Vines, and Trying Times*, singing, "Now I'm done with superstars / And all the tears on her guitar." But as even Joe must have realized, these songs aren't really about boys at all. They're about girls, the topic Taylor has pursued more relentlessly than any other pop artist in history. She's written more songs about girls than anyone, even Paul McCartney, and like Paul, she has nearly no interest in male characters. The boy in a Swift song is usually just a mirror for a girl's experience of self-discovery and self-figuration. He's the blank space where she writes her name. *Fearless* is full of these vibrant girls she's spent her life creating.

"Fearless" will always be my favorite, with those guitars blazing away. This is a girl who feels visible, safe, free to dance beneath the diamond sky with one hand waving free, a star even if her audience is just the boy and the rain. A classic car/girl rock anthem, the kind that actual rock stars were way too cool to write by then. It's crafted with a pro's precision, but she makes it sound like it's all spilling out of her. "I'm not usually this way," sings the girl who is always this way. She *is* the glow off the pavement.

Fearless wasn't a better version of her debut. It wasn't a new and improved version of anything else. She wasn't promising, or impressive for her age. Even over the phone, I could hear it—this was happening right now.

8

EVERYBODY LOVES PETTY, EVERYBODY LOVES COOL

et's talk about Petty Taylor. Some of us love Petty Taylor. Lots of people despise or fear Petty Taylor. A few timid souls might claim Petty Taylor doesn't exist. Good for them. Nice observation, Oedipus. For certain connoisseurs, it's about scoring points against her exes. Others enjoy her celebrity beefs, her lopsided punch-downs, her sometimes-principled conflicts where she crosses the line between "taking a stand" and "making a scene."

But this is mere arithmetic. Some of us love the *calculus* of Petty Taylor.

Here's Taylor speaking at the Tribeca Film Festival, 2022: "People often greatly underestimate how much I will inconvenience myself to prove a point."

OCTOBER 2014: JOHN CLEESE, ON A POPULAR UK TV CHAT program, *The Graham Norton Show*. The Monty Python comedy genius showed up at the BBC tonight ready to spin yarns about his career but maybe a bit underprepared for a conversation with a real-life woman. The other guest is an American singer named Taylor Swift. An odd match, but it should work—the host mentions that they're both cat people. They view photos and trade droll insults about each other's kitties. She calls his a "monster." Chuckles are chucked. All in good fun.

John Cleese explains he's a cat person, not a dog person. "I much prefer cats," he says. "They're unpredictable and cussed, like women! You know?" He waits for her to laugh politely.

You can see the wheels spin in her head—*Comedy legend here, he's eighty-whatever years old, he's making a joke, let this go, smile, be cute, you're in England, laugh politely*. And then you see the wheels click into place—*There are girls watching, of course there are, studying my face to see if I laugh politely*—and she decides to frown. Not a nasty frown. But an on-purpose frown. Then she gives a condescending smile and says, "Ooooh, we don't want to do *that*."

She gets big laughs—slightly too big. Cleese definitely over-laughs, so does the host; it looks almost like they might be relieved. Cut to a commercial.

This chat went viral for a couple of hours that weekend, then vanished and was forgotten. But something about it sticks with me. Who bothers to butt heads with John Cleese? The rest of Monty Python broke up to avoid arguing with him. (As Michael Palin might say, we've seen grown men pull their own heads off rather than see Cleese.) What could be more futile?

I guess it's that futility that fascinates me. For a moment, she really does try to talk herself into being slightly less than Taylor Swift. It doesn't go well.

TAYLOR WILL ALWAYS BE A TOTAL CONTROL FREAK WHO needs to tweak every detail yet hide it all behind a charm-bomb smile. Except when she doesn't. She takes the bait like candy. Unforced errors are a house specialty. She'll air grievances that nobody wants to hear, even when they're totally understandable. She loses arguments she could have won by ignoring them. She delivers comebacks for insults nobody else notices. She will hang a lantern on a nonstory that would blow over in minutes if she just turned off her phone. In 2010, she makes a music-industry journalist named Bob Lefsetz eternally famous with her song "Mean," replying to a negative review in his newsletter, a review that about twelve people would have read if Taylor hadn't given it the oxygen of publicity.

When Nicki Minaj was upset over the VMA nominations in 2015 leaving out her "Anaconda" video, she tweeted that MTV favored "women with very slim bodies." Swift took it personally, posting a reply nobody had asked for: "It's unlike you to pit women against each other." Cue a few hours of online embarrassment, until she gave one of her shrewdest apologies, taking the blame and defusing the situation. "I missed the point, I misunderstood, then misspoke. I'm sorry, Nicki"—that did the trick. At the VMAs a couple weeks later, they joined up for an unannounced duet on "Bad Blood," to the surprise of everyone who'd never seen an award show before. It was a clean, efficient conflict resolution that made them both look good. Neither would make that a habit.

She rumbled with Katy Perry in the early 2010s, after accusing her of trying to steal her backup dancers. "It had to do with business," Swift said. "She tried to hire a bunch of people out from under me." We'd entered a new cultural era: the pop girls were beefing over employees and payroll, not like the days of Hilary Duff and Lindsay Lohan going nuclear over Aaron Carter. But it was a surprise because they were buddies on the come-up. "Katy Perry has so much charisma," Taylor said in 2008. "As soon as I heard 'Hot N Cold,' I fell in love." But when they fell out of love, it brought out their worst, each writing some of their most dreadful songs about the other—singles, no less, "Bad Blood" and "Swish Swish." They made up in 2019, hugging it out for the "You Need to Calm Down" video. Katy not only went to the Eras Tour, she posted video of herself rocking out to "Bad Blood."

For the first six months of 2022, Taylor kept total radio silence, not a peep, until she went online to slam Blur/Gorillaz's Damon Albarn for hinting she didn't really write her songs. That set her off. Couldn't let this one slide. "I was such a big fan of yours until I saw this," she wrote. "You don't have to like my songs, but it's really fucked up to try and discredit my writing. WOW." Albarn graciously replied, "I totally agree with you."

Some of her enemies started out friends. In May 2021, there's no cozier pop couple than Taylor and the up-and-coming Olivia Rodrigo, about to release her brilliant debut album *Sour*. O-Rod calls Swift her hero, but anyone can hear that in her weepy ballad "Drivers License." When she posts "next to taylor on the us i tunes chart i'm in a puddle of tears," Taylor replies, "I say that's my baby and I'm proud." They meet in person in mid-May, snuggling for a photo. Taylor puts a ring on her baby's finger, the kind of ring she wore on *Red*. "She is absolutely the kindest individual in the whole world," Rodrigo gushes. "She gave me this ring because she said she wore one just like it when she wrote *Red* and she wanted me to have one like it." Everybody loves Taylivia. This one is forever.

Yet for some reason, Rodrigo sends a personalized copy of her album to Kim Kardashian. "I just adore you," her note says. "Sending you & ur fam so much love." Kardashian shows her support by posting the note on social media, on May 28, which is a Friday. By sheer coincidence, Taylivia instantly goes from "put a ring on it" to "see you in court," with no explanation from either side. The world buzzes over the mystery of how this friendship ended. All anyone can do is speculate. But Olivia's next album has a song that goes, "I have nightmares each week about that Friday in May / One phone call from you and my whole world was changed." *Rolling Stone* asks Rodrigo point-blank if she's beefing with Taylor. "I don't have beef with anyone," Rodrigo says. "There's so many Twitter conspiracy theories. I only look at alien conspiracy theories."

In February 2024, at the Grammys, Taylor gets up to dance when Olivia sings "Vampire," inspiring hopes for a revival of their Taylivian rhapsody. Swift's next album has a few barbed songs about Kardashian. There's also a song about alien abduction.

IN 2023, SHE WROTE A HIT SONG ABOUT THE ANCIENT CON-cept of karma, then spent the song gloating over all the ways her enemies' lives sucked, which maybe wasn't exactly what the Bhagavad Gita had in mind. As she explained in *Time*, karma means that "Trash takes itself out, every time." But she believes in giving trash a helping hand, fighting battles after they're over, fueling gossip, rumors, bizarre hunches, convoluted theories. She will suck at false humility. She will flunk basic blasé.

My mom had a saying: *You don't have to attend every argument you're invited to.* Taylor doesn't roll that way (and honestly, neither did my mom). She doesn't wait for an invitation—she barges in, without a single doubt that she will make the room shimmer. But sometimes floors are slippery, and nobody takes those *kaboom*s like her. "This Is Why We Can't Have Nice Things" is full of them, in the way she goes "mmm-mmmm" and says, "Therein lies the issue." God, I love that "therein." Her music is full of that Therein Energy.

She sang "Invisible String" in 2020, laughing over the Petty Taylor of yesteryear, back in the days when she used to write songs to skewer her exes in public. "Cold was the steel of my axe to grind / For the boys who broke my heart," she sang. "Now I send their babies presents." She released it the week Joe Jonas became a father for the first time, with his wife Sophie Turner. Taylor sent their baby a present—a gracious gesture showing that they were all mature adults now. Except less than a year later, she dropped "Mr. Perfectly Fine," a *Fearless* vault song roasting Joe for breaking her heart in 2008. Sophie Turner posts an Instagram video dancing to it, saying, "It's not NOT a bop."

In 2023, Sophie and Joe announced their divorce, saying they'd already been secretly separated for six months. A surprise, because just a few weeks earlier, Sophie was out seeing a Jonas Brothers show—wearing a "Mr. Perfectly Fine" friendship bracelet. During the divorce proceedings in New York, Turner moved into Swift's apartment. Let's just say there's a little "therein" in all of us.

9

THE SONGS ON HER ARMS

Taylor used to go onstage every night with song lyrics written on her arms. She'd face an arena of twenty thousand people with the line "I am on a lonely road and I am traveling, traveling, traveling" in Sharpie on her left arm, or "We learned more from a three-minute record than we ever learned in school," or "I am just a dreamer, but you are just a dream," and know that there was a tiny-at-the-time but devoted cadre of fans who were zeroing in on this, keeping track, passing on songs and photos and artists. (Joni Mitchell, Bruce Springsteen, Neil Young, respectively.)

She did this every show on the *Speak Now* tour, in 2011–2012. Sometimes she chose lines from Selena Gomez, or Carole King, or Nicki Minaj. Sometimes she geared it to the specific locale. In Florida, she had "for one desperate moment there, he crept back in her memory," for Tom Petty; Philly got Elton's "'Cause I live and breathe this Philadelphia freedom"; in LA it was "Don't worry baby, everything will turn out all right," for Brian Wilson. In Oklahoma City it was the Flaming Lips. She saved Don Henley for Texas, because she does her research. Some nights she chose country stars like Martina McBride, Dixie Chicks, Kenny Chesney. Other times it was Rihanna or Green Day or Nina Simone or Guns N' Roses, Rachael Yamagata or Death Cab for Cutie or Paramore.

She mixed in up-and-coming songwriters still making their names, or cult figures who presumably picked up some new fans. She had at least one, Matt Nathanson, who later complained that she stole a line from his song "I Saw" for "All Too Well" (and she did, "I forget about you long enough to forget why I needed to," good one), and declared, "She's definitely a fan . . . and now she's a thief." Strong words, but maybe misunderstanding how the folk process works, because sometimes they're the same thing—that's part of how people pass on songs. Music, like poetry, survives by inspiring people to steal it, either in the way they hear it or the way they create it. Music dies when nobody steals it. Love is theft.

The arm lyrics were physical graffiti, a detail that most in the crowd probably wouldn't notice, but one that made each show different. She had music history etched right on her skin. It was a fan gesture that signified the joy of being a fan—wearing your heart on your sleeve, without the sleeve. It was also a way of locating her and her fans in the wider story of pop music—they were all part of this tradition. The night I saw her on that tour, she wore one of her own lines: "May these memories break our fall," from "Long Live."

Joni Mitchell kept showing up on her arms all tour, whether it was "But my heart cried out for you, California," "It's love's illusions I recall: I really don't know love at all," "We love our lovin', but not like we love our freedom," or "All romantics meet the same fate somehow." (It's officially "someday," from "The Last Time I Saw Richard.") Joni looms large in Taylor's music. "I used to cry about Joni Mitchell all the time after a few glasses of wine," she told *Rolling Stone* in 2014. "All my friends would know, once I started crying about Joni Mitchell, it was time for me to go to bed."

Mitchell's 1971 classic *Blue* was formative while Swift was writing *Red*, as she wrote in her journals, later published as part of the 2019 *Lover Diaries*. "I've been thinking about getting old and irrelevancy and how all my heroes ended up alone," she wrote in 2011. "I wrote a song on the plane ride from Sydney to Perth on the Appalachian dulcimer I bought the day of my flight. I bought it because Joni played on most of the record. I taught myself to play 'A Case of You.'" (Mitchell wrote the songs on *Blue* while backpacking through Europe, where a dulcimer was easier to carry than a guitar.) "I wrote a song on it called 'Nothing New' and it's about being scared of aging and things changing and losing what you have." There were rumors of her playing Joni in a biopic, or at least Joni kept claiming, in order to ridicule the younger artist. "I squelched that," she boasted to the *Sunday Times*. "I told the producer, 'All you've got is a girl with high cheekbones.'"

She wore some Joni Mitchell songs in Australia, while also writing "The Lucky One" there, a song often interpreted as being about Mitchell. It's a fantasy about a Hollywood sensation who drops out and escapes from the star-making machinery, so she can retire to her garden—"You took your money and your dignity and got the hell out." But this isn't Mitchell's story at all—she kept making music long after her first wave of fame faded, even fighting her way back to the stage after a near-fatal brain aneurysm. She wasn't precious about her dignity, either—her Eighties included a duet with

Billy Idol. The last thing she would have chosen was getting the hell out. But Taylor just stole what she needed from Joni's story and took it down her own road.

I relate more and more to Taylor the fan. It might be the part of her I identify with most. I identify as a romantic, as a weeper, as a believer in true love, all that stupid old shit like letters and sodas, as someone who hears the music in slamming screen doors and recognizes it as her life story. But damn, I really feel the kinship as a music devotee, someone who listens to everything, but always listens for herself in it. She might expect too much from the song on the radio, might jump into a music style where she doesn't fit, trying to make herself at home. That's how she got started. Country music wasn't her birthright, just something she heard—in suburban Pennsylvania, hundreds of miles from the nearest Georgia star— and claimed as a part of her soul. She treats fandom as an art form. That's why she writes the kind of songs she writes. Taylor the fan is the truest Taylor; everything else comes from that.

10

"ENCHANTED"

have a few dozen favorite moments in "Enchanted," but one of the best comes at the end of the bridge, when she sings, "These are the words I held back, as I was leaving too soon."

"The words I held back": I love that. Picture this girl ever holding back words in her life. I'm sure those words would be very surprised to learn that their relationship with Taylor has ever involved holding back. Especially since ten seconds later she throws in an extra bridge because she has more words, more notes, more ideas than she can fit.

Speak Now was Taylor in the full flush of star power. After the triumph of *Fearless*, she had the clout to write all the songs by herself, so she did, for the first and last time. She also coproduced with Nathan Chapman. It's one of those cases where a star is big enough to call the shots, which has given us some of history's most notorious flops. But not this time. I would argue that *Speak Now* is her secret prog album, with eccentrically shaped songs that run for five or six minutes, lurching all over the place. This was the album that defined the Taylor Swift bridge. These songs take off into epic detours that stretch out like the Golden Gate Bridge, threatening to devour the rest of the song, making you worry how she's ever going to escape from this one, until she jumps back to slam it on home. *Speak Now* is where she turned her bridges into a cult fetish.

Speak Now has its own sound, and she never really went back to it. Now that she proved she could write it all solo, and not only carry the album but blow her first two records out of the water, she figured she didn't need to prove it again. *Speak Now* is a batch of conspicuously unedited songs; nobody in the room was saying, "You've made your point, let's move on." She rambles wildly, like she never did before or would again.

"Enchanted" has its own sonic presence, with its crush-as-hallucination dream-pop vibe. She never revived this sound until "Snow on the Beach," later, yet it inspired not one but two of her signature fragrances, Wonderstruck and Enchanted. It's just her alone with her feelings, letting herself get swept under, into one of those Swift maelstroms where nothing really happens. She meets this fetching gentleman at a party, then stays up all night in her room—wondering if he has a girlfriend, lost in this reverie she's staging. But it's the best night of her life. Nothing makes you suspect she'd be having a better time with her crush actually there. The song really evokes how a teenager dances in a room all alone, conscious of how narrow the walls are, how low the ceiling, how delicately you tread, which floorboards to avoid so you don't wake your folks down the hall. The longer you listen to your feelings bounce off the walls, the more certain you are that you're enduring torments you will remember forever, long after you've left the room. "I'll spin forever," she sings, the opposite of the "Mirrorball" girl who feels doomed to keep dangling in the air, unnoticed by the masquerade revelers below. At the end, when the song is already over, she adopts one of my favorite Prince tricks, overdubbing a duet with herself that becomes the heart of the song.

On the *Reputation* tour in New Jersey, in July 2018, she asked me before the show: "Enchanted" or "The Lucky One"? She knew it was an easy choice for me. But it added an element of stomach-churning anxiety to the show, as if people should be warned that something so cataclysmic was about to happen in the wild-card slot. There had been rain showers off and on that afternoon, but she triggered a full-on thunderstorm with this song. The clouds burst the exact moment she hit the "Please don't be in love with someone else" coda—and nobody will ever convince me she didn't make that happen.

11

EVERY GUITAR-STRING
SCAR ON HER HAND

She began playing guitar as a twelve-year-old kid, with the specific goal of learning to write songs. She'd already owned an acoustic guitar for years but never felt the urge to pick at it. She didn't try strumming her favorite country tunes, not even the ones she sang on her demos. But she decided to start taking lessons because guitars were how songs got written, and with her typical calculation, she felt the songwriting angle would help her snag an album deal. The guitar meant independence. "I could walk into a room and play my own instrument," she said. "I could play songs that I'd written, and that way I wouldn't have to depend on anybody." The guitar would make her an artist—a girl worth listening to.

She began studying with a local instructor—male, of course. "I had this real jerk of a teacher," she said in a 2007 chat with DJ Herb Sudzin. "I was asking, 'So what's the difference between a six-string and twelve-string guitar?' He goes, 'I don't even need to answer that for you, because there's no *way* that you'll be able to play a twelve-string guitar at your age, and your fingers aren't developed enough, and there's no way you'd be able to play it.' The next day she picked out the twelve-string she wanted, and got it for Christmas. "I would play it every single day until my fingers bled. At first it seemed really hard. And then I just realized that if I put my mind to something, then it was really mind over matter, and maybe my fingers *weren't* long enough or developed enough to play it. But I played it." She capped her story with a malevolent cackle. "HAAAA, guitar teacher!"

She gravitated to the twelve-string because it was more work—but also because a man said no. "That's kinda why. For me, I'm really competitive and I'm really stubborn and if you tell me I can't do something, I'm gonna do it."

TAYLOR WAS THE BIGGEST THING TO HAPPEN TO GUITARS IN a minute. The music world had plenty of axemen, from Jack White to John Mayer to Lil Wayne, but this was a girl. She built her visual brand around her guitar, brandishing her rhinestone-encrusted GS6. There hadn't been an iconic female strummer like her since the Nineties girls-with-guitars glory days. Her fans started eyeing guitars—maybe they could learn her songs, or begin writing their own. She was setting a six-string revolution in motion—contrary to all expert predictions about the future of pop music, the hottest up-and-coming phenomenon was a guitarist.

In 2017, the *Washington Post* ran a high-profile article with the headline "The Death of the Electric Guitar." Gibson and Fender were both in debt; so was Guitar Center, to the tune of $1.6 billion. One of Nashville's biggest dealers lamented, "What we need is guitar heroes." But toward the end, almost as a reluctant footnote, there was a twist. "Starting in 2010," the *Post* reported, "the industry witnessed a milestone that would have been unthinkable during the hair-metal era: Acoustic models began to outsell electric."

Yet for some reason, the industry honchos did not see the Swift Effect as a positive development. To them, she was proof that the guitar was finally dead. They weren't sure they wanted this new generation of players. A music teacher in Arizona noted a change at his academy: before, there were a dozen or so girls taking guitar lessons. Suddenly there were ten times as many, with girls outnumbering boys. Andy Mooney, the CEO of Fender, called Swift "the most influential guitarist of recent years." But he didn't mean it as a compliment. For him, this was his nightmare—she meant that this time the game was up. "I don't think that young girls looked at Taylor and said, 'I'm really impressed by the way she plays G major arpeggios,'" Mooney told the *Post*. "They liked how she looked, and they wanted to emulate her."

The obituaries for the electric guitar turned out to be premature—sales boomed during the pandemic. Nowadays, nobody's worrying that the guitar is dead. But nobody's still pretending the girls aren't playing them.

SO WHY DID TAYLOR LOVE HER GUITAR SO MUCH? IT WAS HER constant companion. She clutched it in photo shoots—sometimes proudly, sometimes protectively. She's sung about it from "Teardrops on My Guitar" to "Lover," where she swears her vow "with every guitar-string scar on my hand." It was her chosen symbol of creative autonomy, evoking old-school virtues of authenticity and sincerity. She was no producer's puppet, a *TRL*-bot doing choreographed routines, at a time when the music world had trouble seeing a young pop girl any other way. She was controlling her own narrative, telling her coming-of-age story in real time as it happened—strumming her fate with her fingers, singing her life with her words. But the guitar was also a shield. She arrived in the post-Britney era, a time when pop girls were relentlessly sexualized and objectified, when the bare midriff was a standard part of the image. The guitar was a barrier against the camera's gaze. Her days as a target of harassment started early. In 2008, she told *Rolling Stone*, "I love huggers, but sometimes I get gropers. When it goes beyond ten seconds—that's excessive."

Her axe also let her run around the stage, a girl in motion. She teamed up with Def Leppard for a great 2008 CMT special, her crossover to the metal-mom market with her bang-up version of "Pour Some Sugar on Me." (Her mom loved Def Lep, like so many moms.) It was a major coup for both of them, as she brought Gen X parents into the fold. "I very timidly and politely asked Joe Elliott if I could sing one of the lines in 'Hysteria,'" Taylor said. "And he goes, 'Honey, I've been singin' that song for twenty-five years—you sing whatever you want.'" (Thirteen years later, she twisted that riff into "Evermore.") It might have been different if she'd branded herself as a Piano Girl, in the mode of Vanessa Carlton, Norah Jones, Fiona Apple, or Alicia Keys—she might have seemed more adult, more sedate. Yet you can't really imagine her rise without her axe. A new breed of guitar hero, for a new era.

12

"THE ARCHER"

For me, *Lover* is a grief album. It came out in late summer when it was just sinking in that my mom was not going to get better and that my life as her son was soon to end. So that's how I got to know Taylor's cheeriest album. The goofy humor lifted my spirits—"London Boy" delighted me a lot more than it should have. The miserable songs did not lie. (No, not "Soon You'll Get Better." Left it off my playlist. Maybe someday I'll give it another chance. Probably not.)

Many New Yorkers have a "crying park" and a "crying train," for anonymous and discreet meltdowns, where you're guaranteed not to see anybody you know. Ideally you could take your crying train to the crying park, but city life is rarely that convenient. You can sit on a bench, in the open air, cry as ugly as you want. You might make a spectacle of yourself, but what are horrified-looking strangers for? (My friend had a perfect crying spot: the CD aisle at the Union Square Best Buy, always deserted.) But sometimes you need to find a new park, if it gets too crowded or if you accidentally make eye contact with the old Italian gents on the bocce court. I found a new park in the summer of 2019, in a faraway neighborhood on the other end of the E train.

That's where I sat and listened to *Lover* all day on repeat. The other albums I bonded with there were mostly indie rock— Palehound's *Black Friday*, FKA Twigs' *Magdalene*, Sharon Van Etten's *Remind Me Tomorrow*, Adult Mom's *Soft Spots*, Mannequin Pussy's *Patience*, Lana Del Rey's *Norman Fucking Rockwell*. (Mostly indie rockers who are also Swift admirers.) "The Archer," that was the one. It spoke right to me, as I tried to blend into the background, pretending to be invisible. I flinched every time the line "they see right through me" led into "*I* see right through me!" Like most of the album, it's a song about having secrets that you kid yourself you're doing a great job of hiding, when they're written all over your face. The woman in "The Archer," she believes she's making a bold confession, unaware that her intimacies are already obvious.

My grief felt so stupid to me—I knew this loss was coming my entire life, so why was I so unprepared? Why was I mourning like a rookie, as if I'd never been here before, like this was my first rodeo? I'd learned grief as a young widower, figured I had this drill down cold. But I was caught off guard, which Mom would have enjoyed teasing me about. She was the one who taught me to listen to messy and loud and unmanageable and insistent (and often wrong) (and never tactful) women, in life and in music. When I was growing up, she was relentless about speaking her mind, and always had plenty of mind—the firstborn Irish daughter of a firstborn Irish daughter. In her forties, she began learning to hold back the occasional opinion. You could tell when she was being good, because she would smile and say, "Oh, I am *good*." Always the most outspoken, turbulent presence in my life.

She never taught me to listen to her silence.

My mom didn't want her only son to be a quiet son, so she fiercely encouraged the loudness in me, even when there wasn't much of it. When I gave the eulogy at her funeral, I was showing off for her, since she took pride in having taught her boy to be slightly louder. I'd spent my life showing off for her, making her laugh, rehearsing our next conversations. (No wonder I grew up a fan of outspoken, messy female singers.) Her silence now was something I needed to drown out. So I took music to my bench, steeling myself for bad news. I could spend afternoons with the *Lover* songs and listen to them talk, confident they couldn't see what was wrong with me. These songs were just strangers in a park, witnessing some dark moments I thought were private.

The day after my mother's funeral I listened to *Lover* while walking to a friend's birthday celebration. She was turning thirty and throwing herself a lavish wedding ceremony, where she married the two opposite sides of herself. Mom and I had one of our final conversations about that party, days earlier—I told her the plans because she always loved hearing stories like that, about my friends who were young women on their own, leading their independent lives, having creative adventures, doing the kinds of things that women of her generation never got to try.

Mom had made me promise to give her the details. So I spent the evening collecting stories for her: a Party Connection out in Ridgewood, cool ice sculpture, self-care wedding cocktails, vegan dinner, two massage therapists on hand, Tarot readings in the alcove. The birthday bride pledged her vows, like, "Do you, the healing spiritual seeker, take you, the ball-busting bitch, to have and to hold?" She wanted supportive parent figures there, so she had life-size cut-outs of Bernie Sanders and Cher. Obviously, I didn't mention the funeral, though a few friends knew. I was saving up stories for Mom, for the private conversations we'd be having in my head. But I was really showing off again, working absurdly hard to impress her, proving to us both how poised and calm and unflappable I could be.

The night turned into a karaoke bash, with a room full of women born in 1989, passing the mic to belt every Sheryl Crow hit in the book. One friend, who knew about Mom, made me get up and duet on "Steal My Sunshine." My second karaoke tune was Taylor—I sang "Ours," from 2008, a song that didn't remind me of my mother or death or grief in any way (until then). I walked home long after midnight, walking for miles through industrial North Brooklyn, late September, but instead of listening to my headphones, I sang out loud on a deserted Metropolitan Avenue, as the trucks rumbled by, switching off between "The Archer" and Lana's "The Greatest."

The girl in "The Archer"—she is full of secrets everybody already knows. When she sings, "I never grew up, it's getting so old," she thinks nobody has ever noticed this. When she admits that she has a history of turning her friends into enemies, she's absolutely certain she is the first to mention it, as if her friends and enemies don't laugh about it together. She cannot stop marveling at how skilled she is at hiding her feelings inside, as they dance merrily across her forehead and embarrass the fuck out of everyone else. She's the archetypal cool Eighties friend who comes out to friends who had no idea she was in the closet but try to guess how supportively surprised they should act.

This was my song tonight, for my most pitiful self. Alone on the pavement, breathing in the noxious gas fumes of the Newtown Creek Wastewater Treatment Plant, serenading warehouses and factories. Just another heartbroken son yelling Taylor Swift lyrics at four lanes of late-night truckers and bikers and speed freaks and streetlights, none of them impressed.

"The Archer" needs to be a bombastic rock anthem—it wouldn't work as a ballad, because she's bursting with self-congratulation for finally speaking out loud. It's time the tale were told. She's breaking the silence, confessing her weaknesses, revealing her terror of being trapped alone with herself. She's so eager for strangers to notice the least interesting things about her, doing all her tricks to charm them. They're mortified at how hard she grovels for the crumbs of approval they would have given her for walking away. And there I was, a bereaved man confiding to eighteen-wheelers, under cover of darkness, talking real brave now that no one could hear.

The girl in "The Archer" is one of those Taylor Swift characters who lives in my soul. But she always scares me, because she's the parts of myself I dread. The Archer is confident she's conning everybody, so proud of finally seeing through herself, when she's the last to realize how transparent she is. She laughs too hard to prove she's in on the existential joke. "*You* could stay," she says at the end, suddenly realizing she's running out of time and she hasn't said the most important thing yet. "*You* could stay."

The moment when I'm most terrified of turning into the girl in "The Archer" is the moment I see most clearly that I'll never be anyone else.

THE BRIDGE: THIRTEEN SONGS FROM TAYLOR'S DREAMS

This book needs a bridge, obviously—or is it even about Taylor Swift? These are songs she might have covered, talked about, written on her arms, given her faith and devotion. Some she put on her teenage iPod, or her streaming playlists. Others come from the elders she's been in conversation with for her whole career, in and out of her music. A few just seem to reflect her sensibility in oblique ways. But they all feel like part of her, and part of the bridge she's building.

As she says every night on the Eras Tour: we've come to the first bridge of the evening. She'd prefer that we cross it together.

1. CAROLE KING, "YOU'VE GOT A FRIEND"

When Taylor inducted Carole King into the Rock & Roll Hall of Fame, she called her "the greatest songwriter of all time." They'd always been mutual admirers—a few years earlier, at the American Music Awards, King was the one giving a speech about Swift. But you can't imagine Swift without her where-you-lead worship of King. In the days when she wrote lyrics on her arms onstage, she chose one from "You've Got a Friend," via James Taylor: "You know wherever I am, I'll come running to see you again." Like Taylor, Carole began as a teen songwriter, possessed by an ambition nobody around her could explain. "Her persona on *Tapestry* feels like listening to a close friend intimately sharing the truths of her life so that you can discover the truths of your own," Swift said at the Rock Hall. "It was a watershed moment for humans in the world who have feelings, and for cats who had big dreams of one day ending up on iconic album covers."

2. BEYONCÉ, "IRREPLACEABLE"

In 2008, Taylor shared the contents of her iPod with the world, for a profile in *USA Today*. It's a summary of the eighteen-year-old Tay's everyday soundtrack, with a wide range: Gorillaz, Three 6 Mafia, Jeff Buckley, Pitbull, Metro Station, Oasis, Mannie Fresh, Miranda Lambert, Britney, Paris Hilton. She loved her Nineties rock goddesses, like Alanis Morrisette, Tori Amos, Sheryl Crow, and Liz Phair. She was so into songwriters like Damien Rice (in another contemporary interview she admitted "The Blower's Daughter" made her cry so hard that she ruined a carpet with a purple mascara stain) and Patty Griffin. Kate Bush's "Wuthering Heights," sung by Pat Benatar. Chamillionaire ridin' dirty. She loves it all.

Beyoncé loomed large on Taylor's iPod, naturally. "Irreplaceable" took inspiration from some of the same Nashville queens who got Swift started. "I was thinking about Shania Twain and Faith Hill when I wrote that song," writer Ne-Yo said, calling it "my version of how an R & B country western song would sound." Bey did a countrified "Irreplaceable" with Sugarland, long before "Daddy Lessons" or *Cowboy Carter*.

3. BOB DYLAN, "BOOTS OF SPANISH LEATHER"

I went to Taylor's Tribeca apartment in the fall of 2017 to listen to her new album *Reputation*, for security reasons. (It was the only place where she could guarantee there weren't any hidden microphones.) Two vinyl albums were propped up on the piano where she wrote most of the album: David Bowie's *Diamond Dogs* and Kris Kristofferson's *Border Lord*. She had a book (and only one) sitting on her dining room table: the collected lyrics of Bob Dylan. Could it have been a prop for a visitor's benefit? Sure, why not, yet it didn't sound out of line with *Rep* at all, since her voice was crackling with the surly edge of "Idiot Wind" or "Positively 4th Street." ("You got a lotta nerve to say you are my friend!") As a Dylanologist who's also a Swiftie, I'm aways intrigued by their tight connections. One of the secret coded messages on her *Fearless* lyric sheet, for "Hey Stephen": "love and theft," the title of a great Dylan album from 2001. Of course, she meant the band Love and Theft, whose lead singer she wrote the song about. But "love and theft" still stands as an aesthetic motto for both of them.

"Boots of Spanish Leather" is the Jokerman's most Swiftian song. Two petulant young lovers, in a pissy mood but neither willing to admit it's over, so they stage this ridiculous passive-aggressive fight over nothing and you keep asking, "When exactly does the conversation turn to footwear?" until it drops, and you know what? The breakup was worth it for that punch line. It would fit right in on *Red*.

4. MARY J. BLIGE, "DOUBT"

"It's absolutely foolish to try and sing a Mary J. Blige song, because she is the greatest singer who ever lived," Swift told the LA crowd in 2015. "But this song matters so much to me, and it means so much to me to get to just sing it to you, and I think it could help you if you struggle with the same insecurities that I do." Blige joined her on the *1989* tour to sing "Doubt" as well as "Family Affair." Like so many Mary classics, it's the Queen of Hip-Hop Soul confronting her inner turmoil, wondering if she'll ever stop doubting herself, when all any of us want is to be as cool as she is.

5. CARLY SIMON, "YOU'RE SO VAIN"

If there's a song that sums up Taylor the fan, it might be her child-hood fave, Carly Simon's classic 1972 soft-rock dishfest "You're So Vain." As a kid, she decided her all-time favorite lyric is "I had some dreams, they were clouds in my coffee." Simon rips into her ego-maniac ex, mocking this womanizing, jet-setting, gavotte-dancing, apricot-scarfed Don Juan. But she kept the whole world guessing who she wrote it about. So much of the Swift playbook comes from here.

"When I heard 'You're So Vain,' I just thought, *That is the best song that has ever been written*," she raves in the Red Tour documentary. "That is the most direct way anyone has ever addressed a breakup." She once recalled an entire family dinner the Swifts spent debating who was the real-life guy in "You're So Vain." Mick

Jagger, who's right there singing along? Warren Beatty? Her husband, James Taylor? People have always enjoyed arguing over that mystery and always will. Everybody's got their own theory. But Carly Simon is a true rock star, so she's way too smart to settle the argument. "No, the song is not about just one person," she says in her fantastic 2015 memoir *Boys in the Trees*. "Let's just say Warren Beatty played second base in this particular infield, which he knows so well, but as for who manned first and third—ask the shortstop."

Carly was flying to Palm Springs when her friend peeked in her cup and said, "Check it out—you've got clouds in your coffee." Mick came by the studio while she was recording—Paul and Linda McCartney were hanging out too, along with George Martin and Harry Nilsson. She and Mick sang the chorus in the vocal booth. "I could feel him, eyes wide on me," she wrote. "I was thrilled with the proximity, remembering all the times I had spent imitating him in front of my closet mirror. Only now we were both Narcissus, each desiring the other." Their duet in the vocal booth was pure lust. "I wanted to touch his neck and he was looking at my lips. The electricity was raw . . . Having sex would have actually cooled things off." (Carly *really* knows how to be a rock star.) Mick asked, "How do you know all those chords?" She replied, "I'm just a stuck-up chick.'"

No wonder Taylor grew up dreaming about writing songs like that, wondering, why can't *every* line be "clouds in my coffee"? What if you wrote a whole songbook out of lines that sharp? She was that stuck-up chick. She wanted those chords. She wanted those clouds.

Taylor brought Carly out to sing it in 2013, in Massachusetts. (My sister and her daughter texted me one word around ten—"Carly.") In the Red Tour doc, they cuddle on the couch as Taylor says, "Every girl out there will be thinking of *someone* when we're singing." Carly wears a strategically dipped hat onstage, high-fiving fans; Taylor has rehearsed her Carly stage moves, the way Carly used to rehearse her Mick. After the gig, Taylor asks, "Who *is* 'You're So Vain' written about? Carly hushes her up. "I've already told you, and I've told you never to tell. So *you* know." Taylor holds a finger to her lips. "I *do* know now." She always did.

6. STEVIE NICKS, "SISTERS OF THE MOON"

Stevie and Taylor seemed to get off on the wrong bootheel, with their infamous Grammy duet. That was the last time they were spotted together for a while. But Stevie wrote a warm tribute a few months later. "Taylor is writing for the universal woman and the man who wants to know her," Nicks wrote in *Time*. "The female rock & roll-country-pop songwriter is back, and her name is Taylor Swift. And it's women like her who are going to save the record business."

But Taylor had a real Stevie coup in store for *The Tortured Poets Department*, with an introductory poem by Stevie Nicks, dedicated, "For T—and me." The physical copies had Nicks's handwritten verse, dated August 13 from Austin, musing on the kind of rock-star, romantic mythos she knew well: "She looked back from her future / And shed a few tears / He looked into his past / And actually felt fear." It seemed Stevie was very well acquainted with the classic Tay tropes, touching on Shakespeare, tragedy, loss in the ode to how love slips away.

Swift sang about Nicks in "Clara Bow," in her recollections of her early days breaking into the music business. Men in high places tell her, "You look like Stevie Nicks / in '75, the hair and lips / Crowd goes wild at her fingertips / Half moonshine, a full eclipse." But a few years later, she's obsolete—nothing new—so she gets replaced by someone younger. These men tell next year's in-genue, "You look like Taylor Swift / In this light, we're loving it / You've got edge, she never did." Clara Bow was a 1920s Hollywood movie star, playing the flapper seductress roles in silent films like *Mantrap* and *It*—the term "It Girl" was invented for her. But she got older, forgotten, disappeared from history. Swift loves this kind of story, from "The Lucky One" to "Nothing New," and so does Nicks, from "Gold Dust Woman" to "Mabel Normand." There was always a Stevieness to Taylor's whole aesthetic: her princess-and-castle tales, the flowing gowns of *Speak Now*, the *Folklore/Evermore* forests. Truly sisters of the moon.

But it goes deeper. Stevie Nicks got famous in 1975 with Fleet-wood Mac, with Christine McVie by her side. The Mac had two frontwomen in the same band, both singer-songwriters, rare in the male-dominated Seventies rock world. "Christine and I made a pact the day I joined Fleetwood Mac," Nicks told me in 2019. "She and I said, 'We will never be treated like second class citizens.'" They always had a big-sister/little-sister chemistry: Christine was the sensible, level-headed one (by Mac standards), the older and wiser sister to Stevie's wild heart. Christine sang about limits and compromises; Stevie got swept away at the drop of a top hat. Part of Fleetwood Mac's astounding longevity is that dialogue between them: two sisters with opposite temperaments. "Christine would walk by me—my totally sarcastic best friend. She'd say, "*Soooo*. Writing another song, are we?'" Yet Taylor reflects both sides of that dialogue. She has her Christine side, making rules and setting boundaries, but also her *what* rules? Stevie side. But her Christine is mostly arguing with a Stevie who isn't listening.

After McVie died of cancer in 2022, Stevie mourned in public. At a solo show in Atlanta, she gave a speech thanking Taylor for helping her grieve. "Thank you to Taylor Swift for doing this thing for me, and that is writing a song called 'You're on Your Own, Kid,'" Nicks said. "That is the sadness of how I feel." Stevie heard her long-running Christine bond in it. "We would go back to Fleetwood Mac, and we would walk in and it would be like 'little sister, how are you?'" The song helped Stevie mourn. "When it was the two of us, the two of us were on our own, kids. We always were. Now, I'm having to learn to be on my own, kid, by myself. So you help me to do that. Thank you."

Taylor played Clara Bow live for the first time in Dublin, the night Stevie Nicks attended the Eras Tour. She told the crowd, "A friend of mine is here who is watching the show, and who has really been one of the reasons why I or any female artist gets to do what we get to do. She's paved the way for us." Lightning strikes. Maybe once, maybe twice.

7. KIM CARNES, "BETTE DAVIS EYES"

An oddball cover, from *Speak Now Live*. "There is some unbelievable music that has come from artists who are from LA, did you know that?" Taylor tells the crowd. "I'd love to play you some music that I'm a fan of that's come from LA! Is that okay?" Then she starts strumming the Eighties synth-pop classic, "Bette Davis Eyes." "This one came out in 1981—eight years before I was born!" Nobody seems to recognize it or sing along. The fact that Taylor admires this ode to romantic espionage says a lot—it could be an outtake from *1989*, especially the line, "She's pure as New York snow."

Kim Carnes took "Bette Davis Eyes" to number one, but it was written by the great Jackie DeShannon, a Sixties LA insider who wrote hits for herself and others, collaborating with everyone from Randy Newman to Jimmy Page. (He wrote "Tangerine" for her.) Of course Taylor knows who DeShannon is, and of course she relates to the Bette Davis/Greta Garbo lines. This is a total geek maneuver and she knows it, but she doesn't worry about losing the crowd at all. She sticks with "Bette Davis Eyes" all the way through, fully aware nobody's enjoying this history lesson as much as she is. When she sings "Drops of Jupiter" or "The Sweet Escape," nobody needs any nudging at all.

8. PRINCE, "NOTHING COMPARES 2 U"

"I'm really obsessed with Sinead O'Connor's 'Nothing Compares 2 U,'" she told *Rolling Stone* early on. "When Prince wrote that song, five thousand songwriters put their pens down and went, 'All right, I tried.'"

The Purple One rarely gets compared to her, probably because of his dirty mind, but they have so many affinities. He was the kind of Eighties pop auteur she aspired to be, always unpredictable. A year after *Purple Rain*, he puzzled everyone with the candy-fluff whimsy of *Around the World in a Day* and "Raspberry Beret." "You know how easy it would have been to open *Around the World in a Day* with the guitar solo that's on the end of 'Let's Go Crazy'?" Prince said in 1985. "I don't *want* to make an album like the earlier ones. Wouldn't it be cool to be able to put your albums back-to-back and not get bored, you dig?"

He was the control freak concept-master who built his own private mythology, leaving you to decode his "look for the purple banana" symbolism. She obviously studied his ssongcraft, as in the "Little Red Corvette" synth-pop shimmer of "Dress," or how "Nothing New" tweaks the chorus from "When You Were Mine." But she also seemed to share the way he thrived on hyperfemme energy, surrounding himself with glam sidekicks as extravagantly dolled-up as he was. He turned his life into a lavishly staged High Romantic pageant, populated by lace-and-chiffon supporting players who became chic accessories, as Swift did circa *1989*. He lived in his Girl Squad dream, with Vanity, Apollonia, Sheila E., Diamond, Pearl, as his prototypes for Karlie, Cara, Blake, Dianna, Selena, etc. What is her whole *1989* aesthetic if not basically *Under the Cherry Moon (Taylor's Version)*?

9. THE STARTING LINE, "THE BEST OF ME"

Taylor had the Pennsylvania pop-punk boys on her teen iPod, but obviously never forgot them, because she slipped them into a fantastic song on *Tortured Poets*, "The Black Dog." Her ex forgot to change his phone settings, so she can still track his movements on GPS, and being Taylor, she does. She monitors his footsteps as he walks into a London pub and tries to pick up someone new, until the bartender plays this song and the girl is too young to recognize it. A perfect example of how every song has a role to play in the ongoing emotional pageant.

10. PHIL COLLINS, "CAN'T STOP LOVING YOU"

When Taylor stopped into the BBC's Live Lounge in 2019, she had a surprise up her sleeve: this Eighties pop aficionado did a Phil tribute. "Can't Stop Loving You" is a 1970s obscurity that he turned into a sleeper hit in 2002. As Taylor explained, "I remember driving around Nashville when I first had my driver's license just screaming the words to this song." It's perfect for her—for one thing, it's about crying in the back of a taxi.

11. NELLY, "HOT IN HERRE"

The night the *1989* tour hit St. Louis, T-Swizzle did not pass up her chance to throw down with Nelly, who rapped "Hot In Herre" while the Haim sisters joined her for their "I am getting so hot, I wanna take my clothes off!" back-up dance routine. "She's like a little sister, man, she straight," Nelly said a few days later. "She's just a dope person. She ain't got no ill wills or anything like that, and that's kind of hard when you come from where we come from. You rarely come across those type of people. It's kind of like, Taylor Swift and my granny. Who doesn't love both those people?"

12. PAUL McCARTNEY, "MAYBE I'M AMAZED"

The cosmic Taylor/Paul connection goes so deep. They're both one-off flukes of the universe, wired with similar sets of extremes and contradictions. When she interviewed him for *Rolling Stone*, they jumped right into numerology—he noted how she loved using the number 13, and she asked about how he released his numbered solo albums in years that end with zero. Hopeless, both of them. When they jammed at a 2014 *SNL* afterparty, they played "I Saw Her Standing There," his go-to duet. I once saw him play it live with Springsteen in New York, but twice in a row, with no explanation—as if he wasn't satisfied with the first try. So he made

Bruce play it again, in front of all those people. Can you imagine any other star doing this? Well, yes—exactly one.

But Paul understands how sad songs work. "Music is like a psychiatrist," he told *Rolling Stone* in 2015. "You can tell your guitar things that you can't tell people. And it will answer you with things people can't tell you. So you unload it on yourself, with a guitar."

When Taylor released *Lover*, she did a YouTube livestream with Stella McCartney, promoting eco-friendly merch with no animal products. I couldn't help thinking of Linda McCartney, and how much she would have loved this pushy on-message promo. As Taylor bantered about the album title, Stella casually mused, "All of us are here because our parents had some lover experiences." (It took me hours to recover from that moment, honestly.) There's no rock & roll love story like Paul and Linda, so it's no wonder that Taylor keeps their romance going in her own music. Paul loves to recount all the songs he kept writing in his everyday effort to impress Linda, from "Two of Us" to "Maybe I'm Amazed" to "Jet." "I would come back from a run with a poem to share and having listened, Linda would say, 'What a mind,'" he once recalled. "It's going to make a man feel good, that kind of thing." Years later, Taylor would write an achingly intimate love song for Paul and Linda called "Sweet Nothing," on *Midnights*, where she sings, "On the way home I wrote a poem / You said, 'What a mind.'"

It was touching to see him Fab out at the Eras Tour in the summer of 2024, reveling in Wembley Stadium with his wife, Nancy, and daughters, Stella and Mary, his arms festooned with friendship bracelets and fans dancing all around him. Paul helped pioneer the whole concept that a stadium full of screaming girls was a complex intellectual and artistic adventure (along with everything else it is), so it felt like a passing of the torch. Yet it also felt like a moment he must have seen coming his whole life.

13. LESLEY GORE, "YOU DON'T OWN ME"

Taylor's walk-on music for the Eras Tour: "You Don't Own Me," the 1963 feminist pop classic from Lesley Gore. It booms over the speakers, as a clock ticks down the final minute. Taylor always makes her entrance anthems a big deal, whether it's Tom Petty's "American Girl" on the Speak Now Tour or Lenny Kravitz singing "American Woman" on the Red. But "You Don't Own Me" is the premise of the Eras Tour, of *Taylor's Version*, of her whole career.

Lesley Gore was sixteen when she sang "It's My Party" ("and I'll cry if I want to"), a number one hit, sounding every bit like a nice Jewish girl from New Jersey in the girl-group era. She scored a string of Top 40 hits, mostly about boys treating her like dirt, because "That's The Way Boys Are." She left a dozen or so great songs behind, but "It's My Party" and "You Don't Own Me" are the two that live on, a back-and-forth argument about female autonomy. She was my mom's generation, a people-pleasing ingenue who got chewed up and spat out by the Sixties machine, dismissed as a disposable trifle. She would have been shocked at the idea that years after her death, she'd be singing this song every night to stadiums full of Swifties, as they scream along, "I'm free, and I love to be free!"

For most of her adult life, Lesley Gore felt forgotten, left behind by history, as if her whole life had been a joke. Nobody remembered; nobody cared. In the Nineties, "You Don't Own Me" appeared in a hit movie: *The First Wives Club*, starring Bette Midler, Goldie Hawn, and Diane Keaton. I saw it in the theater with my mom, who'd already seen it with her friends; in the final scene, the ladies sing it while dancing down the street. Gore couldn't believe it. She described the shock in a poignant story from her A&E *Biography* documentary: every day, she made sure to walk her dog by the local theater, right when the movie was ending. She'd lurk there on the sidewalk, unnoticed, just to hear people sing her song on their way out.

In her 1963 heyday, "It's My Party" led to the revenge sequel "Judy's Turn to Cry," where her boyfriend returns, but she didn't fool anyone. Lesley was never gonna get the guy, and he was always gonna walk all over her. You can hear that well of loneliness in her voice, the authentic high-school misery of "I Don't Wanna Be a Loser." I spent a very dark summer of my life listening to a beat-up vinyl copy of her debut album *I'll Cry If I Want To*, twelve songs about tears. Yet Gore always got treated as a joke. She had a guest role on *Batman*, as one of Catwoman's hench-kittens, pleading, "I'm just a rock & roll singer, not a crook!" As Catwoman, Julie Newmar rolls her eyes. "Oh, forget it. You're twenty years old—you're over the hill."

Gore flunked out of stardom, had to grow up. She never got her royalties. As her fan Greil Marcus wrote, "The girl who couldn't be stopped becomes a woman no one wants to hear." But her life changed in the Seventies when she discovered feminism, through her friend and mentor, Congresswoman Bella Abzug. (According to Gore, she was a pallbearer at Abzug's funeral.) In her fifties, she had the courage to come out of the closet—like her peer Dusty Springfield, who did a cover version of "You Don't Own Me." She was in a lesbian couple for thirty-three years, until her death in 2015. Lesley Gore was forced to live up to "You Don't Own Me," in ways she never wanted and wouldn't have chosen. It's the song of a girl who wants to be free. But it also turned out to be the song of a woman who lived and died unowned.

You can hear why Swift hears herself in this song—even on oldies radio, it never fades into the background. Lesley Gore spends the first verse getting her courage up, a quintessential Taylor Shy Girl Talking Tough, except she starts getting carried away, making her demands. No, you can't control her, change her, tell her what to do. She sounds like she can't believe she hears herself speaking up, scaring herself as she shouts, "I'm young! And I *love* to be young! I'm free! And I *love* to be free!" This girl would have to live it out, pay the cost, suffer the tribulations like so many forgotten women of her era, but she kept every vow in the song. This supposed pop trifle was the real deal.

Never in her wildest dreams would Gore have imagined her song would ring out louder than ever in the 2020s, for so many fans hearing her for the first time, after all those years she felt her story was over. It's the ultimate example of music going places you can never predict, but it also feels like a historical reckoning. She's a Marjorie figure on the Eras Tour, a wise woman from the past whose voice becomes part of the show, a living part of the story Swift is telling. What died didn't stay dead.

14

RED

I once found a karaoke bar where the songbook had every Taylor song—even the miserable ones that drag on forever and drive people out of the room. That's right, even "Sad Beautiful Tragic," one of her least-loved songs, a personal fave that she's barely ever played live, because even she couldn't inflict that on people. Two questions hit me at the same time: *What kind of sociopath would sing "Sad Beautiful Tragic" in a karaoke bar?* and *Why am I not friends with this person yet?*

RED CHANGED EVERYTHING ABOUT HER STORY. IT'S WHERE she decided to embrace her love of pop bombast, not that anybody noticed her holding back before. Result? The gaudiest mega-pop manifesto of the decade. The Eurodisco-plus-banjos groove that Shania Twain spent years trying to perfect. The best color-of-romance song since Prince saw the purple rain. The Liz Phair/Ace of Base collab that never happened. No pop auteur could touch her for emotional excess or musical reach—her punk so punk, her disco so disco. When in doubt, she yells "Burnin' red!" and beckons for a guitar solo. I love her song about how exotic it is to hang out with twenty-two-year-olds. I love how she says "refrigerator." I love how she says "drown-i-i-i-ing." I love basically any five-second stretch of this album.

"We Are Never Ever Getting Back Together" was a number one hit, her most shameless pop move to date. She makes fun of indie-rock hipsters, which turned out to be a prescient hint of her future. If this dude was looking for peace of mind in 2012 with "some indie record that's much cooler than mine," he was probably listening to Bon Iver and the National. Consider how easy it would have been to make her ex the bad guy. She could have made him a jerk, a villain, a down-and-dirty cheater. But no, she made it a breakup song where she's as high-strung and clueless as he is, because it's a funnier song that way, and she doesn't mind playing the fool because that's part of feelin' twenty-two. She even lets the guy in this song have friends—which puts her on a higher level of emotional maturity than most of us at twenty-two.

Red reached so far and wide, it made her previous albums sound like the straight country records they weren't, drawing the line that made them "the early stuff." She built dance tracks with producers like Max Martin and Shellback, as in the dubstep drop of "I Knew You Were Trouble." In the disco whoosh of "22," she sings the hook "uh oh" like she invented it, and by the second chorus *she did.* Sometimes she comes on like a world-weary sage. Other times it sounds like all she's learned about maturity is that it's in her dictionary between "Maserati" and "midnight, breakfast at." She wants the electro-fizzle of pop radio, but she wants to go toe-to-toe with whatever she heard in the car that morning. She goes full

Billy Idol in "Holy Ground," nicking the "White Wedding" guitar hook for a song about dancing with herself. "Sad Beautiful Tragic" is Mazzy Swift, going for Hope Sandoval's exact tambourine sound. She takes my least favorite moment in the Steely Dan catalog—the "trouble" whimper in "Dirty Work"—and rubs it in my face until I like it.

Her *Red* tour was a maestro at the top of her or anyone's game. The red sequins on her guitar matched the ones on her microphone, her shoes, and 80 percent of the crowd. She announced, "Thirteen thousand of you opted into hearing about my feelings for the next *two hours*!" She began with "State of Grace," her U2 homage, wearing the Edge's black hat, which made sense since she also had a red guitar, three chords, and the truth. For "Holy Ground" she banged the drum solo on a giant glowing cylinder. "She's rocking out!" the little kid behind me informed her mom. "She's rocking *ooouuut*!"

I will remember this kid the rest of my life. This moment felt like the golden age of something good and right and real.

15

THERE ONCE WAS A GIRL KNOWN BY EVERYONE AND NO ONE: TAYLOR'S CODES

An early radio interview, from 2006: If Taylor weren't a singer, what would she be? "You're gonna think I'm weird," Taylor says. "I would be a cop." The radio dude can't believe his ears. "A cop?" She explains, "Not like a traffic cop but like a *CSI* cop, like a crime scene investigator. I took criminal justice two years, and I really liked it, but not enough to be a lawyer. I like those shows where they've got like the dead body and they wanna find everything. Like *SVU*."

It might seem comical to picture the teenage Taylor fantasizing about chasing crooks and busting perps. But her detective daydream is about solving mysteries, like Sherlock Holmes, Nancy

Drew, Olivia Benson, or Lieutenant Columbo. She wants to be the sleuth, the mastermind. Instead, she became the artist-as-detective, luring the audience into listening like detectives and searching for clues to crack the case along with her.

"Yeah, I'd wanna be like a crime scene investigator," she continues. "Or design dresses."

TAYLOR HAS ALWAYS LOVED SECRET CODES. SHE'S A REAL geek about it. Even at the start, she dropped clues for fans to decode, on her album covers, in her lyrics, in her videos, in her clothes. Even on her debut album, as a sixteen-year-old, she filled the lyrics in the CD booklet with coded messages, with letters capitalized to convey each song's secret meaning. "Teardrops on My Guitar" was "He will never know." "Picture to Burn" was "Date nice boys." "The Outside" was "You are not alone."

"I encoded all these secret messages into every song lyric," she said. "So, if you're reading the lyrics and you're like 'Why is that "A" capitalized?,' it's because it's part of a code. You write down all the letters in order." She added, "If you're really bored—it's a rainy day or something."

She got the idea from the Beatles. "The Beatles did an album where you played it backward—back when they had records and stuff," she said. "You would play it backward and it would say 'Paul is dead, Paul is dead,' all these secret messages and stuff. I can't really do that with CDs because you can't play them backward. So, this was as mysterious and creepy as I could get."

Not even close, as it turned out. She got even more into these mind games as she got more famous. When she drops a new project, the mystery and codes are part of her artistic statement. She's become someone who loves to do a very elaborate album rollout—by the time of *Lover* she was going overboard with the "count the palm trees you can see out the window in this scene from the video to tell how many tracks are on the album" gamecraft. She's built that sort of back-and-forth with her audience, as an interpretive community.

Does she take it all too far? Constantly. "All I started thinking of was, *How do I hint at things, like how far is too far in advance?*" she said in 2021, looking back at the Easter eggs on her first album. "*Can I hint at something three years in advance? Can I even plan things out that far? I think I'm going to try to do it.*" She wants the fans who just like the tunes—but she also wants the weirdos. "I think that it is perfectly reasonable for people to be normal music fans and to have a normal relationship to music. But if you want to go down a rabbit hole with us, come along, the water's great."

She consistently sees her fans as detectives, code breakers, co-conspirators. But her Easter eggs symbolize her sense of mischief, her devious but playful sense of confusing people, and her constant ingenuity as a songwriter. (Ironically, her most pointless mystery ever is her actual murder case, "No Body, No Crime," where the hook is "He did it," which is just cheating.) She has a sly joke about this tendency in the "Anti-Hero" video—after her death, when her family reads the will leaving them nothing, they decide there must be a way to read the will so that it says the *opposite* of what it says. She loves nothing more than to send the audience on a musical scavenger hunt. But she never could have wildest-dreamed how far her fans would take it. Swiftologists can use her music to theorize that she plans her life around solar eclipses, does everything in 112-day cycles because that's how many songs Scooter Braun owned (depends on your math), or assassinated JFK. Yet there's always something lurking there undiscovered even though she gave so many signs. So many signs.

But she tempts people to read the songs autobiographically while always keeping her deepest mysteries to herself. In classic Swiftian form, she wants to be both the mystery and the detective. It's how she keeps her hold on us.

There's a noble tradition of great songwriters creating albums about each other—they fall in love, split up, weep their tears, lick their wounds, but then get to work drowning their sorrows in call-and-response breakup albums. There's a special frisson to albums that dissect the same tragic love affair from opposite perspectives, as in PJ Harvey's *Is This Desire?* vs. Nick Cave's *The Boatman's Call*, or Cat Power's *Moon Pix* vs. Smog's *Knock Knock*. Beyoncé's *Lemonade* vs. Jay-Z's *4:44* chronicles a marriage that stumbled and survived, but with a pained back-and-forth dialogue, including the tantalizing hints about "Becky with the good hair."

And then there's the strange case of Fleetwood Mac, who fully embraced this tradition with *Rumours*. Stevie Nicks and Lindsey Buckingham joined the Mac just in time to begin breaking up and re-breaking up for nearly fifty years. They brought the rest of the band right along with them. As John McVie said, "About the only people in the band who haven't had an affair are me and Lindsey." The Mac seem like the ultimate cautionary tale about why songwriters should avoid falling in love with other songwriters.

That is, unless you're Taylor Swift and Harry Styles. They clearly took this scenario as a challenge. There's no other breakup song tradition quite like the Haylor mythology. Whatever their brief romance meant to them in real life, which neither ever dishes one speck of dirt about—high road all the way, disappointingly—they serve each other as muses, trading songs back and forth. Haylor is a unique case of two brilliant pop brains who keep tossing these paper airplanes back and forth for years—not because there's any bad blood, but just because it's a creative gold mine. They're still at it, as if they just love being part of this tradition too much to let it go. As Harry told *Rolling Stone*'s Cameron Crowe in 2017, "It's the most amazing unspoken dialogue ever."

They're both obsessed with Joni Mitchell—so much so that both learned to play dulcimer because of *Blue*—that perhaps the Haylor folie à deux was inevitable. Nobody ever pulled this move like Mitchell, as she rolled out classic albums full of hate songs, eviscerating the fuckboys of the canyon. I loved *Blue* and Leonard Cohen's *Songs of Love and Hate* for years without having any clue they were singing about each other. She wrote "A Case of You" while he was writing "Joan of Arc"—two of their greatest songs, with no cheap shots or petty spite (saving plenty of that for their other exes). Cohen was the muse who vowed, "I am as constant as the Northern Star," perhaps slightly exaggerating his skill at fidelity, yet they both rose to the artistic challenge with their most intense music. Now that's how romantic misery should work.

She pulled off another great breakup duet with James Taylor, with her *For the Roses* vs. his *Mud Slide Slim and the Blue Horizon*. Some of her funniest JT shade was in her guitar playing, mimicking his signature licks in "See You Sometime," while dunking him for having hit singles ("We're in for more rain") and wearing suspenders. "With my early songs there was so much gossip," she said in

1988. "I wrote a song for James Taylor that mentioned his suspenders. And then on his next album he went and wore his bloody suspenders on the cover! Well, then the cat was completely out of the bag!" (For the record, JT rocked his suspenders on the cover of *Mud Slide Slim* a year before *For the Roses*, so either he had advance warning or he was just fond of those suspenders.)

But Haylor wasn't the kind of relationship you cleansed out of your system in one album, or so it would seem. For her, it meant gems like "Style" and "Out of the Woods." (And "Daylight"?) For him it meant "Perfect" and "Two Ghosts." (And "Daylight"?) Yet neither of them ruined the fun by admitting any of that might have been on purpose. Harry never even uttered Taylor's name aloud, gallantly discreet as always. "It's not like I've ever sat and done an interview and said, 'So I was in a relationship, and this is what happened,' " he told me in 2019. "Because, for me, music is where I let that cross over. It's the *only* place, strangely, where it feels right to let that cross over."

When they met in the spring of 2012, Harry and Taylor were already world-famous paparazzi bait, so they never had much hope of keeping it quiet. (You could even say the world was in black and white, while they were in screaming color.) But they thrived on the chance to play these games in the public eye: twin fire signs, four blue eyes. Even their dates were a tabloid spectacle. Taylor accompanied Harry to an LA tattoo parlor in December 2012, a few days after she turned twenty-three, where she sat by his side and held his hand while he got new ink—a pirate ship, on his upper left arm, right between his skeleton and handshake tattoos. (Same ink as the guy in her "I Knew You Were Trouble" video.) He was wearing a

Rush T-shirt, a mystery in itself—it takes a hell of a confident man to wear a Rush T-shirt on a date with Taylor Swift.

Taylor made him some kind of subliminal presence on *Red*, writing "Treacherous" in early 2012. But *1989* was the real Haylorlode, with the hit "Style," where she raves over the James Dean daydream look in his eye. Just a few months later, One Direction were all over the radio with "Perfect," which ripped the chorus hook of "Style" as Harry vowed, "If you're looking for someone to write your breakup songs about, baby, I'm perfect . . . baby, *we're* perfect!" That "we're" was prescient—as if they could tell that this already-kaput romance was a gift that would just keep giving the world more songs, with enough plausible deniability to cover them both. The catchiest tune on that 1D album was "Olivia," which shared a name with her cat.

"Two Ghosts," was originally written with One Direction in mind, except he realized he wanted to sing it all by himself. "The story was too personal," he said in 2019. He sang about her red lips, blue eyes, white shirt—and most shamelessly, a dance in the refrigerator light. Fans went overboard looking for Haylor symbolism in their music, but there was certainly plenty to dissect. Soon after the two became an item, Styles tweeted two different lyrics from Tender Trap's song "Sweet Disposition," a favorite of hers, then got a tattoo with a garbled quote from the song: "Won't stop till we surrender." The previous line from the song—"Won't stop till it's over"—turned out to be her secret coded message for "Treacherous," which became a highlight of *Red*. So did another song mentioning a sweet disposition.

Both artists kept playing a never-deny, never-explain game. When Cameron Crowe just straight-up asked Harry if he thought Taylor's songs referred to him, he played it cool. "I mean, I don't know if they're about me or not," he said, not totally convincingly. "But the issue is, she's so good, they're bloody everywhere." He didn't begrudge her the songs, because he was doing the same thing. "I write from my experiences; everyone does that. I'm lucky if everything [we went through] helped create those songs. That's what hits your heart. That's the stuff that's hardest to say, and it's the stuff I talk least about. That's the part that's about the two people. I'm never going to tell anybody everything."

Every detail of their romance seemed to fit into a song somewhere. Taylor wore a sweater with a fox on it when they strolled in Central Park; hence "I Know Places," where they're foxes on the run, chased by the hounds of love (or the paparazzi). "Wonderland," Taylor Alison Swift's *Alice in Wonderland* trip, has a Cheshire Cat, since Harry's a cat from Cheshire. One of the best songs on his 2022 *Harry's House* was "Daylight," three years after she ended *Lover* with her "Daylight." When Howard Stern grilled him about it, Styles replied, "We will always wonder." He also sang a snippet of "22" to a fan celebrating a birthday. Haylors worldwide thrilled at the footage of them chatting at the 2023 Grammys; that night, when Harry won his first award, she was the first one in the audience on her feet to applaud. (The "I'm Spartacus" moment of Haylor culture.) Her *1989 (Taylor's Version)* vault tracks had her most explicit (and angriest) songs about him yet, with gems like "Now That We Don't Talk," "Slut!," and "Is It Over Now?" Haylors had enough to craft dissertations. Many did.

More than ever, fans identified as children of the Haylor divorce. (Hell, these two are still battling over custody of Stevie Nicks.) It takes phenomenal amounts of humor, long-range imagination, and message discipline to keep a round of songwriting badminton going this long, not to mention a bloody-minded dedication to mischief for its own sake.

Is it over now? Neither of them will ever give that away. But Haylor is how you turn breaking up into a work of art.

Baby, we're perfect.

16

1989

"This album is not about boys," Taylor Swift told *Billboard* in October 2014, on the verge of releasing *1989*. "It's not about something trivial."

WHEN I HEARD *1989* FOR THE FIRST TIME, I WAS ON HER couch, for security reasons. Her apartment in Tribeca was the only place she didn't have to worry about eavesdroppers. I wondered about my corner of the couch. (Was this where Karlie sits? Lena? Selena?) But the music was a complete shock—a swerve into Eighties-inspired electro-disco. The opening minute of "Welcome to New York" made me wonder if there was static on my headphones. *What* was she doing? What happened to her voice? Where was her guitar? Why didn't this sound like Taylor Swift? And that was before she got to the line about queer kids escaping to the city, where she sings, "Girls and girls and boys and boys!" She was really burning her bridges here. I sat there and wondered, *Am I listening to my favorite artist blow up her career?*

That's exactly what I was listening to. She did not want to be Taylor Swift anymore. It was pure self-sabotage. Nobody was asking her for this. After *Red*, the world was hoping for *Red II: Fifty Shades Redder*, *Red III: Revenge of the Scarf*, or *Red IV: Maple Latte Massacre*. Nobody sane would have advised her, "You know what you should do next? Make an album that sounds nothing like *Red* but exactly like Erasure or the Pet Shop Boys."

Nothing about *1989* made sense. *Red* was a formula she could have milked forever, the country-pop-rock mix that so many artists had spent worthy careers trying to reach. And she was ditching it now? The songs were great—they were Swift songs—but each one made it harder to comprehend why she was depeching her entire mode. There was something wistful about hearing it—I missed her already. But there was a new girl she wanted to be.

Swift had a lot to say about the inspiration she took from the Eighties. "It was a very experimental time in pop music," she said in the press conference livestream where she announced *1989*. I was watching in a sketchy Amtrak waiting room at Penn Station in New York, on my laptop, wearing headphones until a few strangers saw my screen and came over, as did some pigeons. Taylor described the Hair Decade as a golden age she'd missed. "People realized songs didn't have to be this standard drums-guitar-bass-whatever," she said. "People were just wearing whatever crazy colors they wanted to, because why not? There just seemed to be this energy about endless opportunities, endless possibilities, endless ways you could live your life." She applied that to her Eighties makeover. "I thought, *There are no rules to this. I don't need to use the same musicians I've used, or the same band, or the same producers, or the same formula. I can make whatever record I want.*"

The record company wasn't convinced. "They said, 'Are you really sure you want to do this? Are you sure you want to call the album *1989*? We think it's a weird title. Are you sure you want to put an album cover out that has less than half of your face on it? Are you positive that you want to take a genre that you cemented yourself in and switch to one that you are a newcomer to?' And answering all of those questions with 'Yes, I'm sure' really frustrated me at the time—like, 'Guys, don't you understand, this is what I'm dying to do?'"

I spent the Eighties arguing that A Flock of Seagulls' underrated second album *Listen* is far superior to their debut, so this should have been right up my electric avenue. I have been an obsessive tart for new wave synth-pop since the MTV days. But even I had doubts about this move. Yet to everyone's surprise, including mine, people loved hearing her do this. Nobody wanted her playing it safe. Nobody wanted to hear her second-guess what they wanted to hear. Her crazed faith in the audience was totally justified.

David Bowie said that every artist's fantasy was the same: "Crash your plane, walk away."

SHE MADE AN ODD CONFESSION THAT SUMMER WHEN I SAW the *1989* tour at MetLife Stadium. "Real talk, Jersey," she told the crowd. "I haven't always felt like I have real friends, or any friends at all." Her mood didn't seem to fit the upbeat tone of the show. Nobody near me seemed to notice or talked about it later.

1989 was her first album with a real sense of place, set in a New York City of constant romantic intrigue, where the lights and boys are blinding, a metropolis full of Starbucks lovers. She didn't want to play the Sad Girl now. "The risks I took when I toyed with pop sounds and sensibilities on *Red*?" she wrote in her *Taylor's Version* notes. "I wanted to push it further. The sense of freedom I felt when traveling to big bustling cities? I wanted to live in one." That's how Prince saw his musical changeups too. As he said in 1985, he envisioned his albums in terms of "each one going to different cities."

It was the soundtrack to her Girl Squad era. She was accused of dating too much, writing too many songs about too many boyfriends, so she pulled back from dating and made the scene across town with her usual armful of glam girlfriends: Karlie Kloss, Lorde, Lena Dunham, Cara Delevingne, many more. "I had sublime, inexplicable faith and I ran right toward it, in high heels and a crop top," she said in her *Taylor's Version* notes. "Who knew that maybe a girl who surrounds herself with female friends in adulthood is making up for a lack of them in childhood (not starting a tyrannical hot girl cult)?" She felt like the target of slut-shaming, so she stuck with her girl. "If I only hung out with my female friends, people couldn't sensationalize or sexualize that—right? I would learn later on that people could and people would." She loves this whirl, but you can also hear that she worries about whether she really fits here—a teen country star who spent her adolescence on the road, in buses and planes and hotels, fantasizes about belonging somewhere. And part of girldom, as she defines it in her songs, is fighting against that feeling of being a tourist in your own life. That's the reason I will always ride for the much-maligned "Welcome to New York." Anyone can tell she doesn't live there—otherwise she'd have her head down in her phone. It's really a song about not being embarrassed by your own sense of wonder. (It's the kind of NYC ode that can only be written by starstruck outsiders, in the proud tradition of Bowie's "The Jean Genie" or the Clash's "Lightning Strikes" or Joe Jackson's "Steppin' Out.") She doesn't name-check local landmarks—she could switch "New York" to "Spokane," "Des Moines," or any other iambic city without altering a line. She could be anywhere—it's about looking for the romance in the details of wherever you are.

If she wanted to stop gossip about her love life, it was a dubious choice to call one of the best songs "Style," but her high-profile romance with Harry Styles became an inevitable part of how these songs were heard. *1989 (Taylor's Version)* has the best vault tracks of any of her albums, with the anger of "Is It Over Now?," "Now That We Don't Talk," and "Slut!" She's trying to trust in a new romance ("in a world of boys, he's a gentleman") but all too aware of the world's misogynistic disapproval, nothing, "I'll pay the price, you won't." Yet she resolves, "If they call me a slut / It might be worth it for once." "Is It Over Now?" feels like it's part of a trilogy with "The Archer" and "Labyrinth," with that spooky synth-drone ambience. She travels back and forth in time, finding different angles to regard a youthful romance that crashed like a snowmobile. The story is full of blue eyes, blue dressed, red blood, blouses, couches, boats; the jet-set distance of "Come Back . . . Be Here," the scarlet letter of "New Romantics," the NYC coffee of "Holy Ground." This guy turns on the charm for "unsuspecting waiters," just like the guy in "All Too Well" charms her dad like a talk-show host, but it all comes down to a heartbreak that none of these four blue eyes saw coming.

When she leans into her Eighties concept, she gets the sonic details right. "Style" manages to blend nearly every single song on the first Pet Shop Boys album (especially "Love Comes Quickly" and "I Want a Lover," but also "West End Girls" and, okay, *all* of them) for a date between a girl stuck on how hot and intense she is, and a boy who's only a dim reflection of that.

She found a crucial new collaborator in Jack Antonoff, a fellow Eighties geek. Around the time of *1989*, he was making an album with his band Bleachers where he worked with synth-pop originator Vince Clarke. "Modern pop music should just write Vince a check for like a billion dollars for ripping him off all day long," Antonoff told Buzzfeed's Matthew Perpetua in 2014. "Every synth sound, all the low end, that's all stuff Vince created with Yaz, Depeche Mode, and Erasure. It all sounded so much better when he did it." She cheats on the synth-pop concept in the second half—side two, in Eighties terms—with ballads to hedge her bets in case the makeover bombed. She ends it with a killer threesome: "This Love," "I Know Places," "Clean." The underrated "This Love" is her only solo composition, a hushed ballad where she gets down on her knees and sees her own ghost. *1989* is the first album where Taylor encounters ghosts. She'd be meeting more of those.

17

THE WORD "NICE"

hy is Taylor Swift so obsessed with the word "nice"? Songwriters usually won't touch "nice" with a ten-foot cliché. It's an empty syllable-waster. Replace it with "sweet" or "kind" or "wild," even "fine," the song gains more punch. "Nice" just sounds so sappy and insipid. But Taylor *loves* that word. Once you start noticing all the "nice" in her songs, you can't unhear it. She sang it in her first hit, "Tim McGraw" ("It's nice to believe"), but she never outgrew this teen love. She will use "nice" in a chorus. She'll flaunt it. For such a verbally inventive songwriter, it's a real puzzle. Why is she so weirdly fond of such a chintzy little word?

Sometimes she sings it ironically, as in "This Is Why We Can't Have Nice Things." Or a condescending dismissal, like in "Midnight Rain," where she says, "I broke his heart 'cause he was nice." But it's weird how often she means it. In "Begin Again," her date pulls out her chair, and she sings, "You don't know how nice that is / But I do." There's something so oddly poignant about how she shivers in that "nice"—so vulnerable, so unguarded, so first-take, a shy girl describing tricky emotions she doesn't feel safe articulating.

But she loves to play on the self-parodic femme energy of the word, most spectacularly in her massive 2015 hit "Wildest Dreams." Such a grand chorus: "Say you'll remember me / Standing in a nice dress / Staring at the sunset!" That "nice" is doing some heavy lifting. She could have worn a blue dress, red dress, black dress, silk dress, lace dress, crepe dress, new dress, anything. Or hell, even back to "my best dress." In "Bejeweled," the whole song builds up to that hook, "I polish up real . . . *nice!*" She feels ignored, taken for granted, tolerated, after being too polite and compliant, so she's busting loose to go party. Isn't "nice" everything she wants to leave behind?

Does Taylor keep getting pulled back to "nice" because it embodies these fucked-up gender clichés? Is it the demand for female niceness, the way "nice" divides and defines women? Is she reclaiming a word scorned for its girliness? Fighting to liberate the twee? Or just making the best of a trite platitude?

It's a trinket of a word, a cheap piece of tinsel, yet she pins it to her lapel and wears it proudly.

"EVERYONE ALWAYS WANTS TO KNOW IF FAMOUS PEOPLE ARE nice," John Mulaney says in his comedy special *Kid Gorgeous*. "Like Mick Jagger. He came in to host the show. My friends were all like, 'Is he nice?' *Nooooo!*" But why are they surprised? He's spent the past sixty years going out onstage to face worshipful crowds, basking in their adulation as they scream his name orgasmically. That kind of ego rush has to take a toll on anyone's personality. "You're never again going to be like, 'Um, does anyone have a laptop charger I could borrow?'"

Nobody gives a shit if Mick Jagger is nice. The concept simply doesn't apply. Taylor Swift has a very different relationship to nice. It's a gender-coded trap for any woman in the public eye, but she was sixteen, facing the world with an invincible Will to Nice. She was so aggressively the Nice Girl, she raised suspicions that this meant she was Not Really That Nice.

Note: We're not talking about "kindness," or "compassion," or "warmth," real-life virtues that matter on a human level. No, we're talking Nice as cultural currency. Taylor blew up right when smartphones and social media took off—now you were on camera every moment, ramping up the market value of niceness. Katy Perry got famous around the same time. "Everything's different," Katy told me in the summer of 2008. "You don't get any days off. You don't get sick days and you don't get bitch days."

The closest parallel is Bruce Springsteen. Along with Taylor, he's the most extreme case of a star whose charisma is so niceness-adjacent. In his early days, he earned a rep as freakishly nice, beyond the demands of manners or decorum. Fairly or unfairly, people expect Bruce to be that guy. The Boss doesn't get any bitch days off. I don't care how cold-heartedly objective you are as a music aesthete. If you met Bruce in a bar and he said, "You can't sit here" or "Nice ass" or "Don't you know who I am," it would damn well change how you hear "Rosalita."

Yet Bruce had his own attempt at a heel turn, when he fired the E Street Band, fled New Jersey, and moved to Beverly Hills. He was so desperate to break free of niceness, he started talking shit about New Jersey, saying it made him feel "like Santa at the North Pole."

What happened? "I just felt kind of 'Bruced out,'" he said. "I was like, 'Whoa, enough of that.' You end up creating this sort of icon, and eventually it oppresses you."

Taylor knows how that story goes. She's been there too, a few times. When a star is so obscenely wealthy in the currency of Nice, they might wonder, like Bruce, *Is this really me? Am I this icon? Would I exist without it? Am I really a kind, loving, honest person, or am I just Nice? Could I leave the prison of Nice behind me, just go free, for just one day??*

Poor Bruce—he didn't fool anyone. He failed to make a single enemy. He went back to Jersey, got the band back together, nobody was mad. Nobody even remembered those years when he was Bruced Out. It was always going to be different for her.

18

"NEW ROMANTICS"

N
ew Romantics" is one of her most brilliant surprises, a bonus track from *1989*. It's her tribute to the new wave synth-pop poseurs of the early Eighties and how their legacy shows up in the weirdest places. She pledges her kinship with New Romantic movement, which was a formative musical and philosophical influence in my teenage years. I thought I was Taylor's biggest fan, but I never dreamed she had a song like this in her.

Total transparency interlude: The fact that Taylor Swift recorded a song called "New Romantics" is an almost cartoonishly self-parodic combination of my interests. I have never felt so personally targeted by a song, to the point where I wondered if I should be offended. I have seen Duran Duran, the ultimate New Romantics, many times. I wrote a book about my youth called *Talking to Girls About Duran Duran*, because that's how I spent it. I talked to lots of girls about Duran Duran. They were mostly my sisters, but that is beside the point.

When I saw the bonus tracks, I was amused there was a song

titled "New Romantics." Hey, wouldn't it be funny if that turns out to be a new wave synth-pop song full of lyrics stolen from Duran Duran and the Human League, all about New Romantic kids going out to clubs to mope and feel sorry for themselves on the dance floor and brag about how glamorously bored they are and cry tears of mascara in the bathroom? But that's what she had up her sleeve. "New Romantics" is urgent and glittery and perfect, a serial explosion of exquisitely moody synth beats. She throws down the gauntlet with the motto, "We show off our different scarlet letters / Trust me mine is better." Taylor plays it cool vocally—she sings "We're all bored," when boredom is the least Tay of emotions. But then that chorus hits and she's inside the mirror ball, on a floor where the lights and boys are blinding and playing cool won't cut it anymore. Every moment of the song surges with artificial hyperstimulation.

So many friends checked in on me the week that song was released, to see how I was recovering. But the song fit right into her *1989* spirit. As she said, "I was listening to a lot of late-Eighties pop. I really love the chances they were taking. I love how bold it was . . . the idea that you can do what you want, be what you want, wear what you want, love who you want, and you get to decide where your life is going." It's a new style of romance for her, chasing fickle thrills, instead of wishing and hoping for a fairy tale. She vamps it up, especially her jaded sigh after "He can't see it in my face, but I'm about to play my ace-*aaaaah*." It's the new beat as she needs, as she starts up a new career in a new town. This song sums up everything she's trying on *1989*, and everything about the new kind of romantic she's bursting to become.

The New Romantic moment seemed flamboyantly temporary at the time, so it's strange what a long-lived pop mythology it turned out to be. Arty androgynous poseurs like Duran Duran and Culture Club. Mega-glam fops like Adam Ant and Soft Cell, Eurythmics, the Human League and Kajagoogoo and Bananarama and Frankie Goes to Hollywood. And should we mention Haysi Fantayzee? I always do. The New Romantics hold a permanent place in the public imagination. (On *The Tonight Show*, that same year, Cardi B met the comedian John Mulaney and told him, "You look like the Pet Shop Boys.")

The first place I saw the term was *Rolling Stone*, in a dismissive review of the first Depeche Mode album: "Don't look now, but you just missed the New Romantics." At first glance, Taylor Swift might seem the total opposite of the New Romantic ideals of flamboyance and phoniness. She established her adult sound with *Red*. It set her up for an adult country-pop run she had no interest in pursuing. If she wanted to pack stadiums for the rest of her career, all she needed to do was stand onstage with an acoustic guitar. This is not what she chose to do.

Instead, she chose to embrace garish Eighties synth-pop and record a strange anthem for this new phase of her life called "New Romantics." Goodbye, banjos and ballads about autumn leaves and scarves that symbolize innocence; hello, "listened to Orchestral Manoeuvres in the Dark once." The entire *1989* album is her tribute. "New Romantics" was her mission statement. Bizarrely, she left this song off the proper album. That has to be the most shocking New Romantic omission since Depeche Mode left "Sea of Sin" off *Violator*.

After making it a bonus track, she reclaimed this song as a highlight of her *1989* tour and eventually released it as a single. This kind of indecisiveness is very unusual for Swift, normally the most decisive of pop stars, but it suits the song. "New Romantics" is all about muta-tion, all about transition, about setting a wobbly stiletto on a dance floor where you have nowhere to hide. It's a song that's very easy to ridicule and a song that invites ridicule. Adam Ant sang, "Ridicule is nothing to be scared of," Taylor sings, "I could build a castle / Out of all the bricks they threw at me," but it's the same sentiment.

The song comes on like a manifesto, because New Romantics were into manifestos. It didn't just mean wearing frilly shirts; it also meant being pretentious about your frilly shirts. Pretentions were key to the lifestyle, which was why Spandau Ballet chose to call their first album *Journeys to Glory*. The original New Romantics, at the Blitz club in London, wanted to be called "Futurists," but that didn't stick. In 1982, *NME* critic and theorist Paul Morley called Culture Club "post-rock," but that didn't stick either. The name that caught on was "New Romantic," because that label (for which surprisingly few people ever tried to claim credit) struck an emotional chord with its young audience. Like any cool name for a cool thing, "New Romantic" got applied to artists who wanted nothing to do with it, simply because fans found it such a useful shorthand.

As the historian Dave Rimmer writes in his definitive history *New Romantics: The Look*, "'New Romantic' came to connote music that was glitzy, ornate and sexually ambiguous." New Romantics were very eager to be seen as outraging traditional notions of sexual identity and masculine authority. They tended to be the Bowie kids from their towns, they tended to grow up targets of homophobic violence, and New Romantic style was their way of claiming that and flaunting it.

Boy George told me a few years ago, "I grew up with a defensive quality because I'd been picked on at school. I put my head on the style chopping block. At sixteen, seventeen, I walked around knowing I'd get chased and attacked for dressing a certain way—I felt I had an undeniable right to be who I wanted to be. I was always getting attacked by skinheads, mods, casuals, all these tribes." New Romantics taunted the straight world, especially the straight rock & roll world. As David Bowie said, "For Roxy Music and me, mascara was merely the conveyance by which great globs of non-rock flotsam and jetsam were to be delivered."

The ultimate New Romantic stars were obviously Duran Duran, who were the first and probably last band to claim the label in a song, their first single, the 1981 smash "Planet Earth," where Simon Le Bon calls himself "some New Romantic looking for the TV sound." He's sung that line thousands of times since 1981, and never once looked embarrassed. That's just one of the things I revere about Simon Le Bon.

I had a very strange day a few years ago explaining this song's existence to the guys in Duran Duran. It was the summer of 2015, right when they were releasing their excellent album *Paper Gods*. I asked if they happened to know this song by Taylor Swift. Nick Rhodes and John Taylor immediately looked at each other. They'd heard *about* this one but were too wary to listen to it. They were suspicious she might be "taking the piss," as the English say.

But when I brought it up, they were curious. The Duranies knew me as very serious about them and New Romantics in general. They were even more curious about the fact that I actually voluntarily went to a Taylor Swift show. More accurately, they laughed in my face. John Taylor said, "Well, you must have been the guy! The only guy there!" I had to tell him, "Well, I'm kind of used to that from going to *your* shows."

Nick Rhodes admitted he was an admirer. "She's got something, hasn't she?" he said. "She's an original. She's intelligent." But they didn't know what to think about this song. (Nick has boundaries about this kind of thing—he didn't read any of the band members' memoirs and had a policy of never reading books about Duran Duran, including mine.) They were surprised when I confirmed it was a ringing endorsement, sounded just like they'd written it, a song they'd love. And they were intrigued by her journey from country music into synth-pop. For the rest of the day, they kept comparing themselves to Taylor Swift.

John Taylor had a really brilliant comparison when talking about the Duran Duran album *Notorious*, the first album they made as a trio, after two of the original members left.

"Taylor Swift, I don't know a lot about her or her story," John Taylor said. "But I think the big thing is leaving Nashville, right? Both spiritually and physically. There was no going back. Once you've gone to Max Martin, you don't go back to Nashville. But she had a vision for herself that she could exist outside of categories. And I guess we were probably like that with our own sound. We left Nashville. Even before we left Birmingham. In a way, *Notorious* was where we left Nashville."

John Taylor has always been the philosophical member of Duran Duran, so his making such a casually profound spiritual connection to Taylor without even trying made sense. Once a New Romantic, always a New Romantic.

THAT SHE ALSO LEFT THIS SONG OFF THE ALBUM WAS A VERY New Romantic thing to do, especially considering it was the best track. She claims the "New Romantic" sound with a female voice—although the genre was androgynous by definition, most stars were boys in makeup singing to an audience of girls in slightly less makeup. She just wanted to keep changing, showing her range, so she embraced synth-pop as a matter of artistic principle. You could accuse her of being a dilettante, and you'd be right, which makes her the real thing. To be a New Romantic is to be always becoming, always mutating, always overtrying, with a heart of glass or a heart of stone. To be a New Romantic is to be *always* leaving Nashville. Welcome to New Romantic. It's been waiting for you.

19

THE VILLAIN ERA

A sidewalk in Australia: one of the world's most famous street artists, Lushsux, creates a mural in Melbourne, saying, "In Loving Memory of Taylor Swift, 1989–2016." He adds, "No tags please. Respect the dead."

TAYLOR'S VILLAIN ERA SURE DID HAPPEN, AND IT WAS ASTON- ishing how fast she fell from grace and became Public Enemy Number One. The pop culture site *Vulture* called her "the thinking person's least favorite pop star."

How did this happen? She got into a feud with a reality TV star. This was widely hailed as the end of her career. Kim Kardashian— you've heard of her. Perhaps you're familiar with her oeuvre? *Keeping Up with the Kardashians*, on the acclaimed E! network? *Kourtney and Kim Take Miami*? She has a star on the Hollywood Walk of Fame. A big deal. This was a true celebrity cage match. In this corner: Taylor, singer of "Love Story." In that corner: Kim, queen of reality. Wife of hip-hop legend Kanye West. Author of the 2011 novel *Dollhouse*. To the American public in 2016, the choice was easy. RIP, Taylor.

The Kimye feud is the most tiresome, played-out, tedious episode in Swift's life. But it almost ended her. Kim and Kanye were hardly the only issues she had—others were musical, personal, political. But Kimye is the reason these issues coalesced into a full-on Villain Era. Taylor ran afoul of Kanye West, and for a few years there, everything she did was defined in terms of this man and his problems with her. He was the most important relationship in her life, as far as the public was concerned. Taylor's failure to get in his good graces was more than a career coffin; it was proof of her character flaws. If this older man (he was thirty-two when they met, she was nineteen, not controversial or even remarkable then) had grievances to air with her in public, as he did off and on for years, it meant cultural and moral disgrace. Her reputation had never been worse.

THE FEUD EXPLODED IN FEBRUARY 2016, WHEN WEST DROPPED a song about her, "Famous." But it goes back to the notorious incident at the MTV Video Music Awards in September 2009, where Beyoncé was the big winner of the night. Early on, Swift won one of the minor prizes, Best Female Video. West went to the podium, took the mic out of her hand. "Let," that was his word. "I'm really happy for you, and Imma let you finish, but Beyoncé had one of the greatest videos of all time." The camera cut to Beyoncé, shaking her head.

Then MTV abruptly cut away from Swift for a pretaped message from Eminem. It was MTV, not West, who prevented her from saying anything after the incident.

Beyoncé was the champion all night, as everyone knew she would be. She took the top prizes and performed "Single Ladies." When she won Video of the Year, she brought Taylor up so they could share the moment, because Bey was the one person acting like a damn grown-up, as always. (She was twenty-eight, nearly a decade older than Swift, four years younger than West, but she'd been around longer than either, more famous than both combined.) This was the Queen's night, and she made everybody else look like a sniffly child. The next day, Beyoncé was the one in the headlines. Her gesture was hailed as a celebration of sisterhood. She *was* the story. But a week later, Beyoncé wasn't even *in* the story.

The Kanye/Taylor incident created a huge media buzz, especially in New York and LA, where Swift was far less famous than in the rest of the country. Public opinion was all on her side. President Obama called West a "jackass." Oprah sent flowers. Katy Perry posted, "Fuck u kanye. It's like U stepped on a kitten." But the pity was terrible publicity—the most trivializing "poor widdle girl" shit, framing her as if she were Cindy Brady, instead of a serious songwriter who'd just won the Grammy for Album of the Year. Nobody seemed to recognize yet what a disaster this was for Swift.

The Kanye/Taylor screenshot became an iconic visual image. It spoke to male cultural anxiety about the explosion of female-driven pop, which made (and still makes) many men irate, like something is being stolen from them. Kanye was the image of male authenticity speaking truth to girl power. (The only men to perform at the VMAs were Green Day, Muse, and Jay-Z—the rest of the show was

Katy Perry, Lady Gaga, Janet Jackson, Pink, Bey, Tay, and Alicia Keys.) The controversy had nothing to do with the actual award, as Best Female Video is a prize that nobody has ever sincerely cared about. Who won Best Female Video the year before Swift, or the year after? Hell, who won it *last* year? (Nobody did—MTV axed the whole category years ago, and no one even noticed.) The cultural resonance of the controversy was all in that visual binary. But Beyoncé was just erased from the story. Her gesture didn't go viral or inspire memes. Many people have no idea she was right there in the room, or how she chose to respond. Beyoncé's erasure is curious on a lot of levels. She was the wronged party here—it was her night, yet Kanye ensured she went down in history as a loser. Nobody remembers anyone winning a VMA, but she's the only star who famously *lost* one. She was the one with a right to hold a grudge—but she's Beyoncé, and she had other shit to do.

TAYLOR AND KANYE BOTH RELEASED BRILLIANT ALBUMS IN the fall of 2010, their greatest ever so far—*Speak Now* and *My Beautiful Dark Twisted Fantasy*. The rave reviews for these albums didn't mention the VMAs. She wrote a song forgiving him—"Innocent," which she played at the next VMAs. He debuted a much funnier new song, "Runaway." The story already seemed ready to be filed away as a footnote in two of the all-time great pop careers.

But West wasn't ready to let it go. At his November 2010 show at the Bowery Ballroom, a New York club, to launch his new masterpiece *My Beautiful Dark Twisted Fantasy*, he got his biggest cheers of the night when he ranted, "Taylor never came to my defense in any interview and rode the wave, and rode it, and rode it!" He compared himself to George W. Bush, another embattled leader. "There is no leader in history that has been villainized that way and didn't get killed at war or commit suicide, so any man that lives through it deserves one moment of redemption."

Surprisingly, Swift did not have any interest in complaining about West, to the press's dismay. She wouldn't talk about it, despite a media whirlwind for her new *Speak Now*. When she sang "Innocent" at the VMAs, it was the first time she'd mentioned the incident all year; she went right back to not mentioning it. She didn't take the bait when interviewers gave her the aaaw-poor-baby treatment. She simply wouldn't answer the questions. When *New York* asked how the incident affected her, she began, "How it affected me," but then paused. "It doesn't really add anything good if I start victimizing myself and complaining about things."

"Innocent" is a mawkish ballad, with sympathy for a misunderstood and complicated man. "Your string of lights is still bright to me," she reassures him. "Who you are is not what you did." "Innocent" has always been a difficult song to hear, particularly since it's on the same album as "Dear John." When she sings "thirty-two and still growin' up now," it can't help but evoke John Mayer, who was also thirty-two—both men were born in 1977, four months apart. She's nineteen, singing about these men in their thirties who've taken a special interest in her, men who've singled her out and made her a personal pursuit, for reasons she can't see. She feels flattered by their attention, by the trouble they take to be unkind to her. She doesn't doubt that it's her responsibility to understand them. They're men—they are deep, complex, serious, dark, brilliant, mysterious. She is a very young girl. Maybe she can help.

SEPTEMBER 2015, KANYE RETURNED TO THE VMAs TO ACCEPT a Video Vanguard Award for lifetime achievement. In a total surprise, Taylor Swift was on hand to present the award to "my friend Kanye West!" He gave a hilarious, freewheeling, very stoned speech, ending with his announcement, "As you probably could have guessed by this moment, I have decided to run for president in 2020!" A joke, obviously. Taylor raved about Kanye's greatness. "*College Dropout* was the first album that my brother and I bought on iTunes when I was twelve years old," she said. "I have been a fan of his since I can remember." She ended her tribute with the corny but inevitable quip, "All the other winners, I'm really happy for you and Imma let you finish, but Kanye West has had one of the best careers of all time. I'm honored to present the 2015 Video Vanguard Award to my friend Kanye West!"

He sent her flowers the next day. Tay posted the photo with the caption "KanTay2020 #BFFs."

KANYE DROPPED "FAMOUS" IN FEBRUARY 2016, OUT OF THE blue, with the line, "I feel like me and Taylor might still have sex / Why? I made that bitch famous." The video depicted him having sex with her; it had prosthetic naked look-alikes of celebrities, but Swift was the only one targeted sexually. This wasn't a revival of any earlier beef; this was something new. This time, though, everyone was on his side. A few weeks later, when she won a Grammy for *1989*, she spoke about misogyny in the music business, speaking directly to "all the young women out there." Eyes rolled at her speech. "There are going to be people along the way," she warned, "who will try to undercut your success or take credit for your accomplishments or your fame." The impossibility of this night not being about a man—she was the only one who didn't get it.

Kanye claimed that he got her permission for "Famous." "I called Taylor and had an hourlong convo with her about the line," he said. "She thought it was funny and gave her blessings." A strange favor—who asks permission for a dis record? Did Jay-Z and Nas do this? Did Kendrick and Drake? For that matter, did Taylor preview any songs for her exes? The full audio of the phone call leaked years later. Taylor thanks him for warning her—"The heads-up is so nice"—though she sounds unsure why. It's embarrassing how flattered she is when he calls her "a good person and a friend." But she's confused why he's even making this call.

The answer came several months later, in June, when Kim Kardashian revealed that the call had been done for the camera. She posted her own edits on Snapchat, snippets of a twenty-five-minute call. Taylor claimed Kanye never told her about the "sex" line, but the excerpts seemed to prove he did, exposing her as a liar. Kim presented her snippets as "receipts" and tagged Swift with snake emojis. Nobody doubted Kim's integrity, taking her edits at face value. (When the full audio eventually leaked, it backed up Taylor's story.) Eyes rolled again at Taylor's response: "I would very much like to be excluded from this narrative, one that I have never asked to be a part of, since 2009." The request was a bad joke, like her.

"She wanted to play the victim," Kim said on *Keeping Up with the Kardashians*. "It worked so well for her first time."

TAYLOR THEN FELL EVEN FURTHER FROM PUBLIC GRACE IN 2016, for more consequential reasons. She posted a photo on Election Day, standing in line at the polls, saying, "Today is the day. Go out and VOTE." She added a flag emoji.

This was the ghastliest self-inflicted disaster of her career. Pretending to be the only citizen in the republic who wasn't rooting for either side? Not the least bit believable. People wondered if this meant she was a MAGA voter, and Taylor seemed to be going out of her way to encourage this question. She did nothing to suggest otherwise. Taylor has a history of serving her enemies anything they could want, but this time she really threw in the whole Shoney's buffet.

I saw the photo that morning and said, "What the fucking fuck is she thinking?" out loud. The most credible explanation was that she had an opinion that she was eager not to publicize, so most people suspected Taylor was voting Trump and too chickenshit to admit it. Not a stance that would win her friends on the MAGA side—but it cost her a few elsewhere. It took her years to begin correcting that impression. The feckless what-me-worry image as she stood in line, waiting to vote, behind a line of white people—just horrifying.

Clinton had all the female stars rallying behind her, from Beyoncé to Ariana Grande to Mary J. Blige to Gaga to Rihanna. None of them gave a shit if it would hurt their careers. Jennifer Lopez brought Clinton onstage at a show. Madonna did a benefit on Election Day. Nicki Minaj had a single boasting that Trump wanted to deport her. Katy Perry was in New York City at the Javits Center, ready to sing at the victory party. None of them worried about pissing off men. There was still time for Taylor to jump in and get a late pass. Beyoncé waited until the final weekend, then gave a hell of an "I'm with her" speech. Or she could have just kept avoiding the topic. But that photo made her look weak and childish and dishonest. Hillary was still guaranteed to win, obviously, but Taylor had lost big.

The dumbest mistake of her career. And that was *before* 9 p.m. EST. A few minutes later, nobody was thinking about Taylor Swift. Or wanted to, for quite some time.

SHE VOTED FOR CLINTON THAT DAY, LIKE MOST U.S. VOTERS. But her reticence was strange because she hadn't played so timid about Obama in 2008. "I've never seen this country so happy about a political decision in my entire time of being alive," she gushed when he won. "I'm so glad this was my first election." She wrote a victory song called "Change," with a thumbs-up for "the revolution." But in 2016, she was afraid to alienate people, for the reasons her father explains in *Miss Americana*, filmed in October 2018. "Why would you?" Scott Swift asks his daughter. "I mean, does Bob Hope do it? Did Bing Crosby do it? Does Mick Jagger do it?" Andrea Swift asks, "Honey, what the hell?" She isn't talking to her daughter. Complicating the issue was the fact that the controversy was so different for her than it was for any male celebrity. Nobody was asking how Justin Bieber or Justin Timberlake voted; nobody wondered about Drake or the JoBros. Men had the option of neutrality if they chose.

Kanye West voted for Trump. But he chose not to announce it before Election Night, on the advice of his manager, Scooter Braun. In December 2016, he posted a photo celebrating in the Oval Office with the new president, in his MAGA hat.

THIS CONTROVERSY WAS COMPLICATED FURTHER BY A BI- zarre hoax from the alt-right media, claiming that Taylor Swift was seen as a hero by white supremacists. The internet fell for this hook, line, and sinker. The source was alt-right troll Mitchell Sunderland, associated with Breitbart and Milo Yiannopoulos. In May 2016, he published a piece in *Vice* with the headline "Can't Shake It Off: How Taylor Swift Became a Nazi Idol."

The article claimed that there were armies of white supremacists out there who saw Swift as a neo-Nazi icon. The reporter declared that "actual fascists adore Taylor Swift," yet he didn't seem to have any luck actually finding them. He tracked down one, a Nazi blogger, but failed to locate a single other member of this movement. He got his hopes up for a Facebook group called Taylor Swift for Fascist Europe, except that turned out to be a joke. But he still insisted that Swiftie fascists were a real movement, despite coming up slightly short on evidence they existed.

Yet for some reason, the media *loved* this story. It was taken seriously by journalists around the world, who had no trouble believing it and passing it on. For the next few years, it was rare for any article on Swift *not* to mention her Nazi fan base. The zeitgeist desperately wanted a story like this. NPR announced, "White Supremacists Call Taylor Swift an Aryan Goddess." The *Washington Post* quipped, "She doesn't identify as a neo-Nazi." By the time it got to the UK papers, she had a "fervent alt-right fanbase, who have interpreted her blond athleticism as an affirmation of Aryan values." Swift refused to acknowledge it, which would have been the correct move for anyone else. But she had no out—this was a classic "When did you stop abusing kittens?" question. At a saner time, the hoax would have provided some social-media shits and giggles, then burned out in hours. But these were strange days. She was the right villain at the right time.

Would this have happened to any male pop star? Let's just say: it didn't.

KANYE TRIED TO START ANOTHER VMAs FEUD IN THE FALL OF 2016, a few nights after he announced his support for Trump. In Sacramento, he stormed offstage after a thirty-minute rant against Beyoncé, three songs into the show. (The song he'd just begun was "Famous.") She'd swept the VMAs for her epochal masterpiece *Lemonade*, including Video of the Year for "Formation." He accused her of conspiring to steal the award. He declared, "Beyoncé, I was hurt, because I heard that you said you wouldn't perform unless you won Video of the Year over me and 'Hotline Bling.'" He pleaded for Jay-Z not to kill him, saying, "I know you got killers—please don't send them at my head. Just call me. Talk to me like a man!"

It didn't work. The feud never gained any media traction because Bey ignored the whole thing. She always knows the right thing to do.

TAYLOR'S SIDE OF THE WHOLE KARDASHIAN THING? YOU remember—the phone call, the Snapchat snippets, the snakes? That turned out to be true. Crazy, right? Taylor's story was fully vindicated in 2020, when she was solidly back in the public esteem, so it was a little late. But the unedited Kimye call finally leaked on the internet, confirming Swift's story. Somehow, Taylor kept her dignified silence for a couple of days, beyond liking a few Instagram posts, an act of restraint that probably involved a straitjacket. Her silence lasted all the way until Monday afternoon, when she broke down and posted. "Instead of answering those who are asking how I feel about the video footage that leaked, proving that I was telling the truth the whole time about *that call* (you know, the one that was illegally recorded, that *somebody* edited and manipulated in order to frame me and put me, my family, and fans through hell for 4 years) . . . SWIPE UP to see what really matters." She linked to a charity site for victims of the pandemic.

Kim posted her outraged response that night, where she managed to contradict herself in eight consecutive tweets. "I never edited the footage," Kim said. "I only posted a few clips on Snapchat to make my point." Well argued! She also expressed her deep concern about Covid-19.

That's how sick people were of this whole story. It was more fun talking about the pandemic.

"INSTEAD OF ANSWERING"—SHE LIKES THAT IDEA, IN PRINciple. But she can't do it. In 2024, on *The Tortured Poets Department*, she dropped yet another song about this feud, "thanK you aIMee." She capitalized the letters in the title, worried she was being too darn subtle. In August, she tweaked the title to "thank You aimEe," in case anyone missed the dig at Ye. It happened to be the same week *The Tortured Poets Department* blocked his latest album from debuting at number one. Years after she already won this war, she couldn't just walk away the victor. If Taylor were the emperor of Rome, she'd be standing over the smoking ruins of Carthage saying "oh, and another thing" in Latin. After being vindicated in public, Taylor couldn't just walk away a winner. She had to jump back in the ring. She might yearn to be the Instead of Answering girl. However, she is the Answering girl. This conflict will give her no peace as long as she lives.

20

REPUTATION

*R*eputation was the fifth straight time I went into a new Swift album thinking, *I hope she makes the exact same record she made last time*, and the fifth time I've come away thinking, *I'm glad she wasn't taking advice from nimrods like me*. She had everyone expecting (or dreading) an album of celebrity shade, complaining about her famous enemies. Instead, it was an album of adult love songs. Her bait and switch was a work of art.

In *Reputation*, she brings the same level of obsessive detail to mundane adult romance she used to bring to teen crushes. I love how she spends most of the album trying to act jaded and chill, a really sophisticated New Taylor, but then finally gives up and jumps back into Old Taylor hard enough to fracture her ankle. I love the moment in "Getaway Car" when the long-buried Southern Accent Tay suddenly runs back to the phone for that one crazed "Until I switched to the otherrrr side! To the otherrrr si-yi-yide!" I even love how the one big fiasco, "Look What You Made Me Do," is the big statement she probably worked hardest on.

It was another drastic sonic makeover—the same synth-pop premise as *1989*—but chillier, broodier, spikier. "It was nighttime cityspace," she told *Rolling Stone* a couple of years later. "I didn't really want any—or very minimal—traditional acoustic instruments. I imagined old warehouse buildings that had been deserted and factory spaces and all this industrial kind of imagery. So, I wanted the production to have nothing wooden. There's no wood floors on that album."

"I'm sorry, the Old Taylor can't come to the phone right now," she said in the single. "Because she's dead!" But her supposed celebrity concept turned out to be exactly two songs, the awful lead single "Look What You Made Me Do" and the much more likable "This Is Why We Can't Have Nice Things." The moody electronic sound was perfect for winter in the city. I got so obsessed, I taped it on both sides of a cassette, so I could hear it on my Walkman.

But it didn't fit the narrative of what she was about then. It didn't fit the celebrity pity-party image she'd created for this album. It didn't fit the Old Taylor she'd buried, but it also didn't fit the New Taylor she'd gone to so much trouble building. All you had to go on was the music: "Call It What You Want," "Dress," "So It Goes . . .," every last "isn't it?" of "Delicate."

REPUTATION **WAS HER FIRST ALBUM IN THREE YEARS, HER** longest layoff ever. But she didn't let any secrets slip, shying away from interviews. As she announced, "There will be no explanation. There will only be reputation." ("Because I'm melodramatic," she said a couple years later.) It cannot be overstated how bad people expected this album to be. The title and artwork—a black-and-white Swift in dark lipstick, a ripped sweatshirt with five stiches in the shoulder (one for each previous album), blearily gazing through newspaper headlines of her name—it all promised sour times.

And then there were the snakes. All the snake emojis were a direct riposte to Kim Kardashian, America's most trusted snake hunter and brave debunker of Swiftian perfidy. This seemed like the worst possible omen for the new music. Nothing could seem more pointless than the idea of Taylor coming up with clever comebacks in a war of words with a reality TV star—it's not as if they were in the same business or spoke the same language. The first single, "Look What You Made Me Do," was not just her worst single to date but a song that made it reasonable for people to wonder if this was the end of the line.

"Look What You Made Me Do" had the line "I don't like your kingdom keys," a suggestion that she was aiming her bile at one of the two high-profile KKs in her bio. Kim Kardashian was her most high-profile enemy, but she also seemed to be (as far as the public eye could see) fighting with Karlie Kloss, after a couple of years of their extremely high-profile BFFery. There hadn't been any news reports of them falling out. But there was the shirt. At the end of her "Look What You Made Me Do" video, she's wearing a "Junior Jewels" T-shirt decorated with her friends' names, an updated version of the one she wore in "You Belong With Me." Squadologists plotzed at the roll call, from Patrick Stewart (named twice) to Abigail (a month after Swift was a bridesmaid at her wedding) to Selena Gomez (the only one to make BOTH shirts).

But there was a conspicuous blank space: no Karlie. It was mutual: Kloss was currently seen in a new Cole Haan ad campaign posing with her new well-*that*-escalated-quickly pal Christy Turlington. In *Elle* that month, KK gushed, "I am surrounded by extraordinary women—from my mom and sisters to role models like Christy Turlington, Melinda Gates, and Sheryl Sandberg, and many more." What happened?

Taylor and Karlie met in public. "I love Karlie Kloss," Taylor told *Vogue* in 2012. "I want to bake cookies with her!" Kloss hit her back on social media: "Your kitchen or mine?" They dressed alike, walked alike, touched their hair alike, sipped beer in sync courtside at a Knicks game. Karlie posted a beach photo writing "Karlie hearts Taylor" in the sand. But when the Kimye feud went down, Kloss stuck with manager Scooter Braun. The public sightings stopped. When Karlie attended the *Rep* tour—the first time all year they were spotted in the same zip code—they posed for a remarkably awkward Instagram photo. Taylor wore black lace and twisted her wrist so anyone could see the snake ring on her finger. She didn't go to either of Karlie's weddings into the Kushner family. Fans had a field day analyzing *Rep* for clues of their falling out.

Kloss went to the Eras Tour in LA in August 2023. In the most random coincidence in history, Taylor chose that night to announce *1989 (Taylor's Version)*. But she didn't bring her *1989*-era soul mate onstage for the announcement, or wave to Karlie in the VIP seats. That's because the Girl Squad's cheer captain was sitting on the bleachers that night, way up in the nosebleeds. And what song did Swift sing next? "New Romantics"—her song about building her castle of the bricks thrown at her. So long, Daisy May.

People also hunted for clues in the next single from *Reputation*, "... Ready for It?," a week later. Was she talking about this new boyfriend—"He can be my jailer, Burton to this Taylor"? Richard Burton and Elizabeth Taylor got married and divorced twice, which was enough to make them the ultimate 1970s glamour couple—even Sonny and Cher only got to break up once. Their boozy jet-set affair lasted a total of (hmmm) thirteen years, despite the fact that they basically loathed each other. Burton was fond of referring to Liz as "MGM's Little Miss Mammary," while she called him "the Frank Sinatra of Shakespeare." (She didn't mean it as a compliment.) By the time Liz was Swift's age, she was on husband four; Burton was her number five and six. So, Liz and Dick weren't exactly Romeo and Juliet—when they made a Shakespearean film together, it was *The Taming of the Shrew*.

But people suspected she meant Joe Alwyn, a young soft-spoken British actor whose latest role was Queen Elizabeth I's lover in *Mary Queen of Scots*. Burton got an Oscar nod playing QE1's father, King Henry VIII, in *Anne of the Thousand Days*. Nobody knew much else about Joe, but he seemed very good at shutting up, and at the time, that was a major plus in Taylor World.

AND YET *REPUTATION* **HAS SOME OF HER MOST INTIMATE** love songs, exploring what happens when you stop chasing romance and start living your own life. A year into her relationship with Joe Alwyn, largely away from cameras and social media, she was writing long-term love stories that didn't end with a walk home alone. The songs are full of everyday domestic details—spilling wine in the bathtub, building blanket forts. But they also explore a timely question: what happens to your identity when you turn off your phone and stop defining yourself by impressing strangers?

I love all the punk aggro, especially "I Did Something Bad," a flat-out grunge banger designed for a Pearl Jam/Hole/Stone Temple Pilots guitar attack. There's something so Courtney Love when she growls, "I'd do it over and over and over again if IIII coooould." "New Year's Day" is the surprise ending—a quiet piano ballad after so many synth jams. She sings about cleaning up the morning after the party, sweeping glitter off the floor with somebody who makes her look forward to the year ahead. Only Taylor could focus on the least glamorous, most boring holiday in the calendar and find some romance in it. Live, she did it at the piano as a medley with "Long Live," connecting her teen yearning with her adult relationship.

There's a surprising amount of sex ("scratches down your back" is a Tay lyrical first in terms of graphic description) and her first recorded profanity, when she sneers about her exes in the dishy "I Did Something Bad": "If a man talks shit, then I owe him nothing." The aggro really came out in her *Rep* tour, an over-the-top spectacle with hordes of dancers, multiple stages, pyro explosions, and giant inflatable cobras. As Courtney might say, she wanted to be the girl with the most snake. But "Getaway Car," the *Rep* gem that really should have been a hit, began with a poetry recitation that gets at the heart of the story: "And in the death of her reputation, she felt truly alive."

On this album, she's pondering the age-old mystery of—as she sang—why people throw rocks at things that shine. That's not exactly a dilemma only for celebrities. The word "reputation" comes up a lot—in reference not to her public image, but to the far more relatable dilemma of how you surrender your identity in counting the likes and faves you rack up every day, or how many times you look in a mirror, or how much of your neural bandwidth you reserve for the scoreboard on what's wrong with you. That has always been a theme of her songwriting, going back to the high school milieu of her earliest records—she's always sung about girls struggling not to internalize the misogyny around them, from "Fifteen" to "New Romantics" to "Lavender Haze." And as she found out, that struggle doesn't end when you grow up.

Taylor was in court that summer, getting sued for defamation. She had spoken out about an incident from 2013 on the Red Tour when she was groped by a male country radio DJ, backstage, before a show, who reached under her dress in the middle of posing for a photo. It's a horrifying image: her smile, game face on, keeping it together for the camera. She's frozen in a split second of revulsion, confusion, fear, self-doubt, too visible to step back. You can see it in her face: *Is this really happening? Why would he do this, in a public place, where I'm the center of attention?*

She went ballistic as soon as the camera flashed, got him thrown out, got him fired. He sued her for costing him his radio job, but she wouldn't concede a thing. She countersued him for battery and sexual assault, spent the summer in a courtroom instead of on a yacht, testifying and getting cross-examined, saying the word "my ass" more than ever before or since in public. The jury found in her favor, awarding her symbolic damages of one dollar. It wasn't the story she wanted to spend the summer telling, but she didn't back down. She did something bad.

The DJ who groped her just got another job, as men do, moving on to another radio station, another city, a new on-air name. He was now "Stonewall Jackson," because why pass up a chance to be an asshole when you could name yourself after a Confederate general? He could start fresh with a new name, a new reputation.

THERE ARE SO MANY GREAT STORIES ALL OVER *REPUTATION*, but for me, "Delicate" is the best story of all. "Is it cool that I said all that?"—oh, so *now* she asks us. After ten years of brazen overshares, Taylor turns this breathy vocoder whisper into a hyperemotional love song that feels intimate and massive at the same time, flowing like an impulsive confession though it's meticulously put together. Her voice disappears into the groove as she slips off for a late-night rendezvous. Bonus detail: Tay has no idea how bars work. You don't send your date to make you a drink; the bartender fixes it while your date stands there feeling stupid and you check your phone, looking bored. (Welcome to hanging out in dive bars, Tay—you're going to love it!)

But at its heart, "Delicate" is a story about a girl in her room, hearing an electro beat that lures her to go seek some scandalous adventures in the city lights. In other words, the entire story of pop music, in one song.

21

TAYLOR'S VERSION
(TAYLOR'S VERSION)

Taylor Swift will follow through on hollow threats that everyone else would be willing to forget. The most famous example, of course, is one of the biggest elephants in any room at her Holiday House: her whole epic *Taylor's Version* project.

Her former label boss, Big Machine's Scott Borchetta, sold her masters to her sworn enemy, Kanye West manager Scooter Braun, in June 2019. Taylor was outraged. She said she'd been denied the chance to make her own bid on them. She had the money. Both men denied her story.

She trusted Borchetta. Their Big Machine six-album partnership had paid off for both parties. But Borchetta seemed to be nursing hurt feelings about this. His statements about the deal seemed slightly emotional, as did Braun's boasts on social media. Both went out of their way to congratulate themselves on handling a troublesome woman. It was an unusual way for music-biz people to talk about an acquisition.

She got mad about this in public. The populace said, "Right on, Taylor! Go get 'em, Taylor!" Then she announced her response: She was going to rerecord her entire back catalog. All six of her albums. Just redo them from scratch. Put them on sale. Ask people to buy them all over again. The populace said, "Aaah, not so fast, Taylor."

Nobody had ever tried anything like this before. The whole idea sounded so pointless. Tinkering with old albums that nobody thought needed improving? Didn't the busiest star in show biz have other priorities? Didn't she realize how much time and effort she would waste trying to recreate songs she finished years ago? The whole music industry assumed she would change her mind. She had just hit send on a hasty threat without thinking it through. Even hardcore fans could tell you this was obviously—*obviously*—a dumb idea. A bad poker player's stone-cold bluff. In the industry, there was a giggle or two over it.

The business journal *Bloomberg* ran a report a year later, in November 2020, with the headline, "The End of Taylor Swift's $300 Million Fight with Scooter Braun." He'd sold the masters to Shamrock Capital. And that, to the industry experts, was "the end." This story was over. The artist had already lost. In her protests, she was a hypocrite, cynically exploiting the bigger issues of artists' rights, when her real motivation was "personal animus." Her threat was a silly bluff—a girl getting emotional over business.

The *Bloomberg* article, although focused on the financial and legal details, couldn't resist pausing to note, "Swift was never the ideal messenger."

When she dropped *Folklore* and *Evermore*, it was easy to forget this whole rerecording plan was ever mentioned. These albums were a breakthrough for her. And she was supposed to turn backward? Not a chance. She'd moved on to the strongest albums she'd ever made. She was already somewhere new. Why on earth would she want to redo *Red* or *Fearless* now, especially when nobody had any problem at all with the originals?

But then she actually did it, album by album, adding vault tracks to each new edition. As you know, this plan was wildly successful on a creative and commercial level that even she (maybe? for a hot minute?) couldn't have imagined. If she says she can do it, she can do it. She don't make false claims. The project cost her enemies fortunes, making them look like chumps. SZA called it "the biggest 'fuck you' to the establishment I've ever seen in my life, and I deeply applaud that shit." The rerecords sound even better than the originals—her adult voice adds so much firepower—and listeners prefer them. (Except for "Holy Ground," on *Red*. That one didn't turn out right—too much synth buzz in the mix, instead of the percussive acoustic guitar that makes the original go. Maybe we will have to wait for "Holy Ground: Taylor's Version of Taylor's Version.")

The *Taylor's Version* project has gone down in history as a mastermind's triumph, so nobody will ever admit they thought it was the dumbest move of her life, even though practically everybody did as soon as she announced it. It's like Dylan going electric or Stravinsky premiering *The Rite of Spring* or Radiohead making *Kid A*—who wants to admit they booed? Who wants to be one of the clods who thought this plan was a self-defeating mistake, a faceplant of epic proportions? Well, I'm that clod, and I wouldn't dream of lying to you about it. I thought this whole idea was a total waste of her time. I never believed she'd go through with it, not for a minute. I prayed Taylor Swift would change her mind and back down. I might as well have prayed for a unicorn to sneeze on me.

A minute into *Fearless (Taylor's Version)*, it went from "She shouldn't be doing this" to "Wait, she's really doing this?" to "Damn, it would have been a tragedy *not* to do this." That whole tormented backstory—that wasn't the story anymore at all. People not only enjoyed the mix of old songs and new songs—they seemed to love the whole idea of it, a woman hitting her thirties and revisiting her previous selves. You hear old stories she left behind but also the parts she tucked away and saved for later. "You All Over Me" is a song she wrote about getting clean, at eighteen. She kept it a secret, then six years later released "Clean," then released this one six years after that. In "Mr. Perfectly Fine," she sings about a guy who's "casually cruel" but decided to save that line for a better song.

In all the *Taylor's Version* remakes, there's one vocal detail that I especially savor. It's on *Red (Taylor's Version)*, deep in "We Are Never Ever Getting Back Together." There's a little extra venom in the way she snarls, "Trust me." You have to wonder if it comes from those nine additional years of hearing men ask her to trust them.

THERE'S A SCENE IN *THE GODFATHER PART II* THAT SOME- times reminds me of Taylor. Michael Corleone wants to shoot Hyman Roth at the airport, a pure petty move. Roth already lost in his feud with the Corleone family, years after double-crossing them. Now he's an old man, in frail health. The doctors give him six months to live. He's getting deported back to the United States. As soon as he gets off the plane, the Feds will arrest him and lead him off to die in prison. But the Godfather wants him shot at the boarding gate, right before the handcuffs go on. His consigliere,

Tom Hagen, tries talking sense to him. "Is it worth it? I mean, you've *won*. You wanna wipe everybody out?"

Al Pacino munches on his apple. "I don't feel I have to wipe out everybody, Tom," he says. "Just my enemies, that's all."

THAT'S A KEY PART OF BEING TAYLOR: THE CONSTANT REVIS-ing of the self *IS* the self. She will go on rewriting her songs, remaking her albums, revisiting the Taylors she's already been, sometimes giving them a little compassion, sometimes going to them for forgiveness. She will keep looking back at her old stories from her changing perspectives, the way adults do, reflecting on former relationships as cruelties or even crime scenes, or recognizing former catastrophes as cosmic jokes.

That's clear from her songs and her long-running musical evolution. This is just the most outrageously giant-scale example of how she's constantly remaking herself, constantly revising her younger self, constantly rewriting the story of her life.

Self-revision is a habit with a bad reputation. Take her favorite Romantic poet, William Wordsworth, who did such massively brilliant and influential work in his youth, then spent the last forty-five years of his life fixing his old poems, mostly correcting them for theological or moral errors. He made none of his poetry better this way. For younger poets like Shelley, Byron, and Keats, Wordsworth was the innovator they idolized but also their most dreaded symbol of creative burnout—their worst-case scenario was growing old enough to write drivel like *The Recluse*. (All of them accidentally evaded this fate by dying young. He outlived them all.)

He finished his epic masterpiece *The Prelude* in 1805 but kept working on it—and watering it down—for the rest of his days. He capped his career decline by inspiring the funniest bad review in history, by Francis Jeffrey in the *Edinburgh Review* in 1814, beginning with the famous words "This will never do." Jeffrey recommends "making up our minds, though with the most sincere pain and reluctance, to consider him as finally lost to the good cause of poetry." What went so wrong? "Long habits of seclusion, and an excessive ambition of originality," he laments, "can alone account for the disproportion which seems to exist between this author's taste and his genius." That sums up how *Taylor's Version* should have failed, except it didn't.

Taylor has always been revising her songs—soon after she dropped her debut, she rerecorded "Picture to Burn" for the excellent reason of editing out a homophobic joke. The biggest tweak was the long-anticipated change in "Better Than Revenge (Taylor's Version)," where she changes "she's better known for the things she does on the mattress" to "you're like a moth to the flame and she holds the matches." Whether you happen to hear the original song as slut-shaming or Swift-shaming, it's a big change, and you could argue she's selling the song short. First, the tired old moth/flame line is exactly the kind of cliché that the young Swift came along to destroy—she held her 2010 self to brutally high standards, so it seems a little mean to put such an embarrassingly lazy line in her younger mouth. But also, there's the sense that the song is a scene in the melodramatic inner life of an extremely unlikable narrator, a petty teen narcissist, and making fun of this narrator is the whole point of the song.

But still, you can't begrudge a songwriter who changes their mind about a song that means something to them. Every time Bono sings "Pride (In the Name of Love)," he changes "early morning,

April 4" to "early evening," because that's when the MLK assassination happened—he knows better now. Should Bono serve a life sentence of retelling the story inaccurately? Of course not. When Morrissey started singing "How Soon Is Now" for the first time in many years, he made an excellent change, dropping the line about standing on your own and wanting to die. Now he sings, "You go and you stand on your own / And you leave on your own / What a biiiig surrrrrpriiiiiise!" I like the song better that way—a lot better—but I get you if you think that's a loss for the song or a betrayal of an adolescent bond you felt with it. Yet there's no law saying that as an artist you have to go on singing words you don't mean.

But on another level—is this CHEATING? Well, yes, of course it is. So what? It's very Swiftian to keep tinkering with her past. Anything less would be betraying the girl she used to be.

THE WHOLE *TAYLOR'S VERSION* PROJECT IS A TRIBUTE TO her unmitigated chutzpah and the role it plays in her ever-evolving artistic identity. Nobody had ever tried such a thing before—much less tried such a thing seven times. But Taylor was out to regain control over her catalog, her whole legacy, her whole history.

It's standard for legacy artists to rerecord lame versions of their hits to take advantage of a new label deal (like when Modern English remade their classic Eighties one-shot "I Melt with You" in 1990) or for TV commercials (like when Modern English redid the same hit for Burger King, addressing the love song to his Whopper). It's not regarded as respectable work. A more subtle and discreet classic-rock tradition is the live album, after veterans snag a more lucrative contract. When Simon and Garfunkel did their hugely popular Central

Park reunion album in 1982, it might have been a sentimental gesture, but as critic Robert Christgau noted, it was also "a corporate boondoggle—a classy way for Warner Bros. artist Simon to rerecord, rerelease, and resell the catalog CBS is sitting on."

Such subtlety is not our girl's way.

The big question is, why? What possessed her to put so much labor and time into this? What does it mean for her to go back and revisit these stories and feelings? What does it say about her lifelong project of growth and evolution? She not only reclaimed her art but also demonstrated her enduring connection with the audience that flipped for *Fearless* in 2008, the audience that joined her to re-explore it in 2021, and the many devotees these songs had picked up along the way.

Taylor's Version goes way beyond the corporate intricacies that spurred her into it. Indeed, the Scooterific backstory already seems like a footnote to a major creative project. The *TV* phenomenon symbolizes Swift's unwavering commitment to creative autonomy—a refusal to let external forces define her artistic narrative. By revisiting and rerecording her early albums, Swift not only reclaims ownership but also offers a nuanced reflection on the way her music has evolved over the years—the way she has.

22

"CRUEL SUMMER"

"Cruel Summer" was the hit for a summer that never happened. It took years to become the beach bombshell it was always meant to be. "Cruel Summer" has taken a strange path through time, in ways its creator couldn't have foreseen. But in 2023, it crashed the radio, carried by the Eras Tour and fan demand—a four-year-old album track that blew up into a top ten hit, as the once and future summer banger fulfilled its destiny. It's a song that snuck out through the garden gate and went places nobody expected.

As soon as she dropped *Lover*, everybody wanted to know: why the hell didn't she make "Cruel Summer" the lead single, in time for June? She picked "ME!" when she had this ready to go? This was the obvious hit, a synth-pop fever dream cowritten with Jack Antonoff and St. Vincent. It had nothing to do with Bananarama's 1983 hit, except that they shared the same great title and the same spirit. She was clearly holding it back to be the summer soundtrack of 2020, in time for her scheduled Lover Fest stadium shows. But the pandemic killed those plans. A year later, she was going the opposite direction with *Folklore*, leaving this song stranded. Whatever future it had was forgotten—the wrong cruel, for the wrong summer.

She packs so much bittersweet pop lust into three minutes, creeping out the window for a secret rendezvous, until she's crying in the back of the car. For the first ninety-eight seconds, it's merely a perfect Taylor Swift song. Then for the bridge, she takes off into a deranged greatest-hits album's worth of choruses from songs she hasn't written yet. She feels ashamed of her secrets, yet proud of how ashamed she is, until she yells her dirtiest secret out loud: "I love you, ain't that the worst thing you ever heard?" But make no mistake, she loves her secrets more than she'll ever love this paramour.

It had a place of honor on the Eras Tour, early in the show. Every night that summer, just to seal our fate, she made a celebration out of the "Cruel Summer" bridge, declaring, "We have arrived at the very first bridge of the evening! Now I would prefer that we cross it together!" As the phenomenon of the tour kept building, it lifted this song onto the radio. It reached the top ten, where it smoldered all year long. It finally hit number one—in January.

"Cruel Summer" is her ultimate window song, and not just the way she sings "Killing me slow, out the window." There's so much mystery in the erotics of windows in Taylor's song—she's got a Keatsian obsession with the kind of desire that doesn't dare use the door. Heading out the window, she feels a rush that she doesn't feel when she gets wherever she's slithering off to. These lovers keep it on the hush, but that's the attraction, the sub-rosa thrill. She's seduced by the window, more than by anything on either side of it. She sings, "I don't wanna keep secrets just to keep you," but she's drawn to thresholds, gates, liminal spaces, any portal to a forbidden place. Windows are for tapping on, tossing pebbles, hiding in the curtains. Doors are for confessions and transitions. She loves sneaking into gardens, weddings, yacht-club parties, and beds.

There's so much breathless excitement in how she sings "I snuck in through the garden gate / Every night that summer just to seal my fate." The rock & roll philosophers might have warned her that *windows are for cheaters, winners use the door*, but she prefers the window every time. Whatever's on the other side, she'll take her chances. Devils roll the dice, angels roll their eyes.

23

THE LEAD SINGLE

he Taylor Lead Single is a tradition in itself. When she's introducing a new album, she likes to drop a lead single that confuses people. Or sometimes it makes them gnash their teeth and bang their heads on the carpet in despair. She never likes to give away her secrets too early. She loves to throw everybody off the trail. Sometimes she gets a sadistic kick out of picking the weakest song on the album as the lead single.

Why does she like to mess with fans' minds this way? She just does. The most quintessential Taylor Lead Single is "ME!" from *Lover*. And not just because it's terrible, though that helps. It can't stop showing off how terrible it is, in a very specific Taylor Lead Single way.

Keep in mind: the first song Swift debuts from a new album is always an outlier. It's a big thematic statement addressing her public image; it talks about the celebrity Taylor, rather than the personal one. "Innocent" from *Speak Now* (not a single, but the first song she introduced at the 2010 VMAs), "We Are Never Ever Getting Back

Together" from *Red*, "Shake It Off" from *1989*, "Look What You Made Me Do" from *Reputation*, "Anti-Hero" from *Midnights*. Some of these are perfectly great songs—but they end up not telling us a damn thing about the album.

"Look What You Made Me Do" was the most cleverly misleading version of this. It made everybody worry *Reputation* was going to be a whole album of celebrity shade, which turned out to be just a couple of songs. (Whew!) But arguably it did the job *too* well—it created a false narrative for *Reputation* that was hard for people to shake, even after they heard what was (pretty damn explicitly) an album of love songs. "ME!" is far more playful, but it still pokes fun at her image, with lines like "I know that I went psycho on the phone." You know she's swerving hard back into Old Tay mode post-*Reputation* when she includes a line about a boy running after her in the rain calling her name.

Her obvious role model for choosing a lead single: *Thriller*. Strange as it seems now, when Michael Jackson was preparing to drop *Thriller* on the world in 1982, the first song he released was . . . "The Girl Is Mine." So, everybody thought *Thriller* was going to be a whole album of saccharine ballads using the word "doggone." Even his duet partner Paul McCartney found it baffling—as he admitted, "You could say it's shallow." (And this from the ex-Beatle who released a 1972 solo single of "Mary Had a Little Lamb.") That's part of why "Billie Jean" stunned the world—nobody was ready for it, because he'd fooled us all with "The Girl Is Mine." That's how MJ wanted it. And that's how Taylor likes to do it, too.

"ME!" might be the most quintessential Taylor Lead Single of all time. It hits all the tropes. Every Taylor Lead Single is required to have a spoken-word moment: "Spelling is fun" joins the tradition of "I mean, this is ex-HAUS-ting," "The old Taylor can't come to the phone right now" and "The fella over there with the hella good hair." That's another way she follows the strategy of "The Girl Is Mine," since the highlight of that song was the Michael/Macca dialogue, e.g. "Paul, I think I told you I'm a lover, not a fighter!" (The "ME!" video has a neon sign that reads "Lover," a hint to the still-unannounced album title.) "ME!" was the first song in her catalog in all caps or with an exclamation point, a surprise given that she's a very exclamation-prone type. For the video she brought in Brendon Urie from Panic! at the Disco, and speaks French, yelling, "*Je suis calme!*" It made the song feel like a kiddie tune: The pastels. The rainbows. The first unicorn in her videos. The video also debuted her new cat, Benjamin. So much panic. So much disco. Not much song. "ME!" sounds even more bizarre if you go back and listen knowing she was on to *Folklore* less than a year later. She sure swerved violently from "Spelling is fun!" to "If I'm dead to you, why are you at the wake?"

Nobody enjoys a strategically elaborate album reveal like our girl—no pop star in history has ever made it such an integral part of her artistic evolution. She is never going to make the same album she made last time, and the lead single is never going to spill the tea on where she's speeding now. A hint, yes; some clues, *bien sûr*; the full story, never.

24

I'M NOT ASLEEP, MY MIND IS ALIVE: *LOVER*

Around the time she made *Lover*, Swift had LASIK surgery. Her mother made a video of Taylor post-surgery, in a druggy stupor after anesthesia. Taylor struggles with a bunch of bananas in the kitchen, until she finally gets one loose. She starts to cry. "That wasn't the one I wanted!" When Mama Swift takes it, Taylor whimpers, "But it doesn't have a head!" She shuffles to bed, moaning, "Sometimes it doesn't go your way." If you're the kind of person who finds her unbearable, this clip is your Exhibit A.

Taylor can't even stay awake eating her banana. When her mom catches her nodding off midbite, Taylor denies it. She insists, "I'm not asleep, my mind is alive."

LOVER WAS THE END OF A DECADE BUT THE START OF AN AGE. These days it's her most popular album, her biggest hit, still riding high in the charts. It's the only time she set out to make an album she knew everyone would like, with her pinkest artwork and pinkest tunes. It was also her first summer album, with a new aesthetic of psychedelic pastels. She was now into butterflies and rainbows and moonbeams and roses, like a flower child in a Jimi Hendrix song. Closing down her twenties, kicking off her thirties, she wanted to gather all her previous selves from the past decade. *Lover* revived the twangy country ballads people thought she didn't feel like writing anymore, as well as her perky electro-disco and pop gloss. It had her cozy slow-dances, her yearning introspection, her feminist rage, her Southern accent, her English accent, her brilliant ideas, her terrible ones. She even busted out her "refrigerator light" accent, one of my favorite Swift voices.

Fans gnashed their teeth over the lead single, "ME!," but a week later, she dropped "The Archer" and then "Lover," two different sides of her music. In Prince terms, if *Speak Now* was her *1999* and *Red* was her *Purple Rain* and *Reputation* was her *Parade*, this was her *Sign o' the Times*, the one where she puts all her best tricks on one album. After *Reputation*, it was strange to hear her work so hard to make everyone feel at home. But she also wanted an industry win. *Lover* was radio-friendly, retail-friendly, award-friendly. She made a point of scheduling it in time to make the Grammy deadline, a concession that earned her nothing. (*Lover*, the bestselling album of 2019, got one nomination, the same as the Grateful Dead, the Alan Parsons Project, and Jimmy Carter.) Right before it dropped, she attended a gala with her date Abigail Anderson, the high school friend of "Fifteen," a callback to the *Fearless* era.

Lover was her "Saturn return" album, as she headed into the new decade. Many great songwriters get introspective when they're facing thirty, whether it's David Bowie on *Low*, Joni Mitchell on *For the Roses*, Carole King on *Tapestry*, or Al Green on *The Belle Album*. For one who falls in and out of love on a roller-coaster rhythm, *Lover* is an album about *being* in love, which is both scarier and harder to write songs about. "Cornelia Street" is one of her best. It's the same plot as "Holy Ground"—a girl in New York City, surrounded by a city that reminds her of a lover she misses before he's even gone. But in "Cornelia Street," it's not that magic "first day" anymore. She's trying to hold on and make it real. How do you keep your ground holy when you actually have to walk on it and live there? That's the question she asks all over these songs.

All over *Lover*, she's in touch with her younger self, every corner of her borrowed and blue heart. "Miss Americana & the Heartbreak Prince" revisits the high school days of *Fearless*, just as "Daylight" updates the young-adult romantic of *1989*. The girl who made her mom drop her off a block away from the party is now driving her mom to the hospital. She begins the title song by boasting how she's wild and carefree enough to leave the Christmas lights up until January, a whole week. But when she takes that vow of eternal devotion in "Lover"—with every guitar-string scar on her hand—the soul mate she's really embracing is her chaotic self.

A *LOVER* MOMENT I ALWAYS KEEP COMING BACK TO IS THE VIDEO FOR her title song. So many beautiful images in "Lover." A madly-in-love couple. A happily-ever-after marriage. A fancy dinner. A Christmas morning where it turns out this is all happening inside a snow globe, the same one she sang about at sixteen in "Mary's Song," another love-is-forever ballad from more than a decade earlier.

The lovers snuggle together at the dinner table. Yet every time I watch, I get distracted by the cranberry sauce. I am haunted by this cranberry sauce. This happy, loving couple, enjoying a romantic dinner for two, with pasta . . . and cranberry sauce? Why in God's name is there cranberry sauce at this dinner table? These two people don't even LIKE cranberry sauce. They're not eating it. It's just sitting there untouched, two whole jelly stacks of the stuff, fresh out of the can. Who puts cranberry sauce on spaghetti?

Oh, the power of Taylor's mind and the decisions she makes. Honestly, nothing about this bill of fare makes sense—a bowl of cherries? A pizza with fried eggs? Yet Taylor and her beau don't even notice. They're too busy gazing into each other's eyes. (She's also distracted by his "salad dressing" dad joke, which is admittedly a good one.) Maybe that's what Taylor is trying to tell us. Maybe this cranberry sauce symbolizes what true romance is all about. Maybe love doesn't have to be burning red. Maybe it doesn't even have to be golden. Maybe the definition of romance is a sad little plate of cranberry sauce, sitting forlorn on the table, that you don't even see because you're just so in love.

These lovers are lost together in a dream. They are ignoring their dinner. They are ignoring their cranberry sauce. They're in a world of their own, oblivious to any distraction. To the rest of us, they might look ridiculous. But they're not asleep. Their minds are alive.

25

FOLKLORE

What makes *Folklore* her best album? It isn't just "August." Or even "Mirrorball." It's the way the songs keep evolving the longer you live with them. It's the way she builds her most labyrinthine fictional universe. The way "This Is Me Trying" shrugs off the despair with the hilariously tight-lipped punch line "I have a lot of regrets about that." The way your ears perk up at the piano intro to "The Last Great American Dynasty," then you realize this is the kind of album where the closest thing to a lighten-the-mood bop is the one about the lonesome widow who spends her nights pacing the rocks on the beach, after her party guests have drunk all her champagne and left her behind.

It's the guitar on "Illicit Affairs." The strings on "Seven." The Wordsworth trip of "The Lakes"—six years after "New Romantics," she goes Old Romantic. All three "try"s in "All I do is try, try, try." The way her usual stories about sneaking around and hiding secrets hit so different in the pandemic, when the shame of craving other people's company felt like a scarlet letter. The way she enters her thirties with an album that dusts anything she did in her roaring twenties. But more than anything, it's the giddy moment at the end of "August," when it sounds like the song is over, you think she's finally going to drive away with her head held high, but she can't stop herself from circling back for just one more "Get in the car!" Okay, fine—maybe it *is* "August."

Folklore happened in a time of isolation. "I survived mostly on wine and watching seven hundred hours of TV every day," she said, "but I also made *Folklore*." Swift had to cancel her summer Lover Fest shows, so she threw herself into her new secret project. Mostly just acoustic guitar and piano, in collaboration with the National's Aaron Dessner and her wingman Jack Antonoff. The three were never in the same room—they made the album long-distance. She left her regular life and identity behind. "I was not just a millennial woman. I was a Victorian woman writing with a feather quill on a piece of parchment that's tea-stained with one of those candle holders."

I woke up the morning of July 22 to a text from Team Taylor that this surprise album was coming. I kept listening to this insanely great album—her most drastic musical swerve yet, picking up her acoustic guitar for a stark goth-folk sound, with her most ambitious storytelling. As she explained in her prologue, "In isolation my imagination has run wild and this album is the result, a collection of songs and stories that flowed like a stream of consciousness. Picking up a pen was my way of escaping into fantasy, history, and memory." I listened to it for eighteen hours straight. All these brooding ballads. All these lost, haunted, broken characters. This was an entire album of Track Fives. Most of all, the album is full of outcast women. So many heroic witches, widows, crones, madwomen, on *Folklore*, lurking in haunted houses, hiding in the attic.

I spent the plague year with *Folklore*, like many people. (Nobody knew at this point *Folklore* was about to get a sister album five months later.) She released *Folklore* on cassette—it sounds great on tape because side one ends with "This Is Me Trying," so right after the music fades, with the final *ka-chunk* of the tape stopping dead. I found a spot to listen to it, in a North Brooklyn nook by the river, sitting on the rocks behind the sewage treatment plant. Nobody else ever went near there since it's a polluted urban dump, but it was a secluded sanctum to sit, watch the ducks, see the dirty water ripple as it got dirtier, sing along with *Folklore*, feeling all these misfits and outcasts, watching the sun set over Manhattan. Not the most romantic listening environment, but the right one for these songs.

Folklore was the one that impressed people who didn't like her (and who went back to not liking her later). The writer Sean Howe has defined the concept of the "Nebrasterisk," where a divisive artist makes an album that even skeptics can admire. It's such an outlier in the catalog, it appeals to nonfans. The classic example is Bruce Springsteen's *Nebraska*, his stark acoustic detour, recorded in his kitchen on a 4-track. Hipsters who looked down their noses at the Boss and his cult could make an exception for this one, without worrying about getting accused of being a fan. ("I can't stand Springsteen, BUT . . .") U2 had their *Achtung Baby*, the Stones had their *Exile*, Drake his *If You're Reading This It's Too Late*, Nirvana their *In Utero*, AC/DC their *Back in Black*. *Folklore* was Taylor's Nebrasterisk, so anomalous that it could be heard without the usual baggage. It was harmless to like, since you could dismiss it as a fluke.

Since she figured she wasn't going to be touring with these songs anyway, she gave up on doing anything for the radio, anything rah-rah or stadium friendly. She just made some coffee, sat at the piano, and let her mind wander into some dark places. She let her fictional characters tell their own stories. A scandalous old widow, hated by her whole town. A scared seven-year-old girl and her traumatized best friend, wishing they could run away and be pirates. A ghost watching her enemies at the funeral. Recovering addicts. A fumbling teenage boy. Three of the highlights—"Cardigan," "August," and "Betty"—depict the same love triangle, from all three different perspectives. Other songs tell both sides of a story: "The 1" and "Peace," or "Invisible String" and "The Lakes." "This Is Me Trying" is the disturbingly witty tale of someone pouring her heart out, to keep herself from pouring more whiskey.

Part of the *Folklore* effect was how it drove me back to *Reputation*; I kept both albums playing heavily in a back-to-back rotation. They're such perfect spiritual twins, her two most extreme albums, with their black-and-white covers, used as bookends for the rainbow that is *Lover*. (Just like how Prince used *Parade* and *The Black Album* as bookends around *Sign o' the Times*.) It's the first album where she doesn't laugh. No country moves, no first dates, no "Taylor visits a city" song. She'd done music like this before—the vibe is close to "Safe & Sound," the rootsy gem she did with the Civil Wars for the *Hunger Games* soundtrack in 2012. But this is even more extreme. "This Is Me Trying" is full of lines I need to get carved on my tombstone—except it would take three or four tombstones to hold them all. "I was so ahead of the curve, the curve became a sphere"—what a math flex. Taylor once said that when she sang "Mad Woman," she'd get a facial expression she called "the FolkGlare," and you can picture that in any of these songs.

You can listen for years trying to puzzle out all the intricately interwoven narrative details. "Mirrorball" is about the same nervous dance-floor poseur of "New Romantics," six years later, except in this song, she's the disco ball that reflects everyone's most desperate insecurities. "Illicit Affairs" is another tale of infidelity, with two secret lovers who have to meet in a parking lot. (It can't be the same parking lot from "Fearless," can it?) She's got old folks, little kids, teenagers. In "The Lakes," she walks in the footsteps of William Wordsworth, the Romantic poet who essentially invented the kind of introspective writing she does, wandering the Windermere peaks of the Lake District with Coleridge.

But the Teen Love Trilogy is the heart of the album: James, Betty, and Augusta, with a crucial walk-on for Inez. The songs tell different versions of the same romance. James is the first time she's sung explicitly from the perspective of a boy, which naturally means he does a lot of apologizing. But it's telling that his opening line is "Betty, I won't make assumptions . . ." When she slips into an explicitly male-coded narrator, the first thing she imagines about male privilege is the right to make unchallenged assumptions. It's a self-consciously designed heartland rock saga. "Betty" even kicks off with a harmonica solo straight from Bruce Springsteen's boy/girl/car classic "Thunder Road"—a song that begins with the slamming screen door where Taylor began her own story in "Our Song." She's all three of these lovers, and they're all her. For the big climax, James shows up at her party, ready to beg for forgiveness. (Was James listening to *1989* in the car? Because he follows all the advice she gives in "How You Get the Girl," and it works: they kiss on the porch, in front of all her stupid friends.)

But for me, the hero of the story is Augusta, who doesn't even get mentioned by name—whatever Betty and James want from each other, Augusta is cooler than either of them. Taylor reveals her name in her live album, *The Long Pond Studio Sessions.* "I've been in my head calling the girl from 'August' 'Augusta' or 'Augustine.' I've just been naming her that in my head." Could she be the Romantic poet Augusta Leigh, Lord Byron's sister? That would fit the nineteenth-century poetic scene of "The Lakes."

The way Swift sees the story, Betty ends up getting back together with James. But even if Betty might get the guy, Augusta gets the song, and that's a win for Augusta. The triangle ends with Augusta stranded at the mall, still waiting in her car. But she makes that parking lot behind the mall sound like the most romantic getaway on earth.

 26

"MIRRORBALL"

M irrorball" is such a fragile little shiver of a song. My favorite version is the one she sings in *The Long Pond Studio Sessions*, her live album from November 2020. Before she sings "Mirrorball," she sets the scene. "I just saw, you know, lonely disco ball, twinkly lights, neon signs, people drinking beer by the bar, a couple of stragglers on the dance floor," she says. "Just sort of a sad moonlit lonely experience, in the middle of a town that you've never been."

Never been? Hell, some of us call it home. But she evokes this maudlin bar scene, tapping into the same loneliness Paul Westerberg described in the Replacements' "Swingin Party," which was the best song about a mirrorball. She turns into the disco ball looking down on the dance floor, wondering why everybody else is having such a good time and wondering what that's like. She reflects everyone's secret anxieties, the ones they're dressed up to hide, as if she's in the same club as "New Romantics," but from a different angle, feeling even more vulnerable and exposed. It's a cautiously unflashy ballad about feeling a little too loud and a little too bright, wondering if everyone's staring at her flaws but feeling invisible anyway.

This "Mirrorball" dropped in *The Long Pond Studio Sessions*, the film special she released four months after *Folklore*, playing these songs with Aaron Dessner and Jack Antonoff, all in the same room together for the first time. She's deep in the woods, in a rustic cabin at the National's Long Pond Studio in New York's Hudson Valley. She explains how "Mirrorball" came to her in quarantine. "I wrote this song right after I found out all my shows were canceled," she says. "I'm like, 'I'm still on that tightrope, I'm still trying everything to get you laughing at me.'"

She premiered *The Long Pond Studio Sessions* over a Thanksgiving weekend when most American families (like mine) were separated by the pandemic. It was also exactly ten years after the cozy flannel Thanksgiving that gave us "All Too Well," and for any viewers who might not pick up on that detail, she spends much of the sessions wearing plaid shirts, while she and her two guitar boys get lost upstate, surrounded by the autumn leaves. She soaks up the rural ambience, talking on the porch or in the yard beside the barn. But for such a miserable holiday, she luxuriates in the melancholy of the songs. "When lockdown happened, I just found myself completely listless and purposeless—and that was in the first three days of it." So she sat down to write, and these songs just spilled out. She dreamed it all up in isolation—"rockdown," as her pal Paul McCartney liked to call it. "There's something about the complete and total uncertainty about life that causes endless anxiety," she says. "It turned out everybody needed a good cry, as well as us."

"Mirrorball" has the enveloping warmth of the electro-ballads on *Reputation*, but it's suffused with the tingle of anxiety. It's the same desperation she sings about in "This Is Me Trying," the other "I want you to know" song on *Folklore*, as well as the other *try-try-try* song. "On *Folklore* there are a lot of songs that reference each other, or lyrical parallels," she says in the studio. "And one of the ones that I like is the entire song 'This Is Me Trying' then being referenced again in 'Mirrorball.'" Dessner and Antonoff stretch out on guitar, nailing the rainbow-in-the-dark mood.

The whole *Long Pond Studio Sessions* spell ended just a few weeks later, when she dropped *Evermore*. So it's a misfit in the *Folkmore* story—dangling between two albums, not belonging anywhere. All her broken *Folkmore* characters are different facets of her mirror-ball, and they all have a light to shine.

27

"MARJORIE"

In December 2020, Taylor Swift released *Evermore*, her surprise sister album to *Folklore*. "To put it plainly, we just couldn't stop writing songs," she said. "To try and put it more poetically, it feels like we were standing on the edge of the folklorian woods and had a choice: to turn and go back or to travel further into the forest of this music. We chose to wander deeper in."

Evermore came just five months after *Folklore*—and just a few weeks after she redefined the *Folklore* songs with her *Long Pond Studio Sessions*. She wrote "Happiness" just a week before the album came out. *Evermore* is a companion to *Folklore*, but with some of the same stories: "Coney Island," her duet with Matt Berninger of The National, sounds like the "August" girl left her small town, forgot James and Betty, moved to New York, found a hipster boy, figured everything would be different in the big old city, then found herself trapped in the same story all over again. When you're a grown-up, they assume you know nothing.

Like *Folklore*, *Evermore* is all cathartic beauty, an album full of ghost stories and haunted houses. But the most heartbreaking moment is "Marjorie," Taylor's tribute to her late grandmother. It's not just the centerpiece of a stunning album. It's a song that ties up all her favorite obsessions into a story of love, death, and grief. It's one of the best things she's ever done. It's a new peak for her as a storyteller, with the key line "What died didn't stay dead."

She wrote "Marjorie" with Dessner, as a tribute to her real-life grandmother Marjorie Finlay, an opera singer who passed away in 2003. When she announced the album, Swift called it "one starring my grandmother, Marjorie, who still visits me sometimes . . . if only in my dreams." She brings in Finlay's voice at the end—when she confesses, "If I didn't know better / I'd think you were singing to me now," we hear Marjorie's soprano voice singing along with her.

Just as *Evermore* is a sister album to *Folklore*, this is a sister song to "Epiphany," the stark ballad of her grandfather Dean and his World War II combat experience on Guadalcanal. (Like "Epiphany," "Marjorie" is placed at track thirteen.) Dean was her father's father, Finlay her mother's mother, but they're immortalized in songs about living with the dead as you grow older and feeling their spirit in your bones.

Swift made a video full of family footage, where Marjorie seems right at home in front of a camera, in her bouffant and lipstick. In one scene, she shares a piano bench with her granddaughter; Taylor is just a toddler, but Marjorie is already showing her where to place her hands on the keys. Marjorie Finlay was a classically trained virtuoso who grew up in Memphis, singing in her high school choir in Mexico, Missouri. She majored in music at college, and in 1950 won a talent contest to go on the radio show *Music with the Girls*. Her career took off in Puerto Rico, where she lived with her husband after some time in Havana. She sang with the Puerto Rico Symphony Orchestra and at the La Concha Room at San Juan's Caribe Hilton. She also hosted her own TV show. In a news clipping from her hometown paper, as seen in the video, she says, "My Spanish was bad enough to be funny and the audience loved it. I became a sort of straight man for the show's MC."

Her granddaughter made a life in music, the kind of life Marjorie could only dream about. But she didn't live long enough to see her become a star. As Taylor sings, she died with "All your closets of backlogged dreams / And how you left them all for me."

The song's power comes from Taylor's hushed vocal over the seething electronic pulse, a nod to Steve Reich's *Music for 18 Musicians*. (Bryce Dessner orchestrated it, with vintage synths and strings, and Bon Iver's Justin Vernon is on background vocals.) "I should have asked you questions," Taylor sings. "I should have asked you how to be / Asked you to write it down for me / Should have kept every grocery store receipt / Because every scrap of you would be taken from me." Taylor makes her small-town diva of a grandma the star she must have always wanted to be. (Another news clipping from the hometown paper: "Her parents had always discouraged her from doing supper club work, and she accepted the engagement only after assuring them that 'this will be very dignified.'")

The night Taylor dropped *Evermore*, she wrote to a fan on YouTube, "I have about 50 fav lyrics but right now it's . . . 'Never be so kind you forget to be clever. Never be so clever you forget to be kind.'" That's the advice her grandmother gives her in this song. She wishes her adult self could have learned even more from this wise woman. But that's part of grief—the work is never done, and there's never a resolution to the story. (Even if the album had "Closure"—the least Swiftian of concepts.)

Like so many songs on *Folklore* and *Evermore*, "Marjorie" is about living with memories, learning from the dead, carrying on with the hard work of grief. When she announced *Evermore*, she explained, "I wanted to surprise you with this the week of my 31st birthday. I also know this holiday season will be a lonely one for most of us and if there are any of you out there who turn to music to cope with missing loved ones the way I do, this is for you." *Evermore* was a true holiday album, complete with "'Tis the Damn Season," in the midst of a winter full of isolation and fear. "Marjorie" became a highlight of the Eras Tour, as Taylor sang along with her grandmother's voice booming over the speakers. "She would have loved to sing at MetLife Stadium," Taylor said after performing the song in New Jersey. "I guess technically, she just did."

Elsewhere on the album, Swift sings, "My mind turns your life into folklore / I can't dare to dream about you anymore." But on *Folklore* and *Evermore*, turning the lives of our loved ones into folklore is how we keep them alive—it's how we ensure that like a folk song, their love will be passed on. "Marjorie" is about communing with someone you've lost and trying to hear the story they always wanted to tell you. It's about holding on to the memories so they will hold on to you.

28

"RIGHT WHERE YOU LEFT ME"

Right Where You Left Me" is Taylor sitting in a restaurant, alone in her corner, where she always goes to relive the worst moment of her life. The restaurant where she got her heart broken. It all happened so fast. The boy across the table told her he was leaving her for somebody else. Not a pretty scene—mascara running, glass shattering. A long time ago. But she's still trapped in that moment, paralyzed in the past. Everybody moved on. She stayed there.

She can hear what people whisper at the other tables. "Did you ever hear about the girl who got frozen?" they ask each other. "She's still twenty-three, inside her fantasy, how it was supposed to be." Every time she wails, "You left me *noooo*," she sounds more desperate, over Aaron Dessner's obsessive banjo hook. The banjo keeps urging her to get out of there, but she can't move. It's the only Swift song with an actual cry for help—twice—and it's a powerful sound. Scary shit.

"Right Where You Left Me" is a bonus track on *Evermore*—a decade after she was feeling twenty-two, she writes the ultimate song about feeling stuck in twenty-three. It's the hardest-charging song on the album, a riff that repeats insistently, which is why it would sound great in a metal arrangement. It's designed to be heard at the end, after you've already been through the wringer for an hour. After the somber piano notes of the title song, you might feel ready for a blanket, a pillow, a mug of herbal tea, but that's not what you get. There's a little more emotional brutality in store for you. "It's Time to Go" follows with rational advice from a well-adjusted adult, telling you to cut ties and leave the past behind. She could be talking to the girl in "Right Where You Left Me," telling her, "Sometimes giving up is the strong thing / Sometimes to run is the brave thing." Of the two voices at the end of *Evermore*, she's the one to listen to and take seriously. But the other is more fun. (In terms of topics where you trust her expert advice, "knowing when it's time to go" comes between "galactic astrobiology" and "blind-folded machete combat.")

In "Right Where You Left Me" she already knows it's time to go but doesn't care. She can't stop revisiting the same table, paralyzed in the past. She sets the scene so you can see the napkins and count the silverware. I always hear it as the same restaurant as "Begin Again," where they had their first date. He pulled out the chair for her, and he didn't know how nice it was, but she did. Now she's back at her corner two-top, where the regulars know to leave her alone. The staff probably groan every time she walks in.

She knows people can see her—that's a crucial part of the experience. She loves that people are gossiping about her, fork-pointing behind napkins, saying, "What a sad sight!" She needs witnesses.

She wonders about the guy out there, with his wife and kids. He might not even remember her. (This breakup wasn't "Champagne Problems" for him—more like "Midnight Rain.") The hushed dream sequence in the middle where she imagines a happy ending that won't happen—it's the saddest one since Bruce Springsteen's "Downbound Train." If you've had any kind of traumatic grief experience, you know this scene well—returning to where it went wrong, dreaming of how it could have been different. She's still twenty-three, inside her fantasy.

Most of the time, when I hear "Right Where You Left Me," I'm sitting at that table, collecting dust. Other times I'm the other people in the restaurant, witnessing the scene, as we do when we hear the song. Embarrassed spectators, trying to eat dinner, hoping they never turn into her.

But sometimes I'm the banjo. While she sits frozen, the banjo tries to warn her, telling her it's not too late to escape, plucking that riff like it's tugging her sleeve. *Let's go. Let's move on. Grab the check and never come back. Run for your life. Get moving while you still can.* The song ends, and we have no idea if she ever listened.

29

MIDNIGHTS

At the end of *Lover*, her biggest album, Taylor had a lesson she wanted to share, in the spoken-word envoi at the climax of "Daylight." "I wanna be defined by the things that I love," she announced. "Not the things I hate. Not the things that I'm afraid of. Or the things that haunt me in the middle of the night."

Guess she got over that shit. Daylight had a good run, but she moved on with *Midnights*, her album of insomniac misery. Taylor announced the album as "the stories of thirteen sleepless nights scattered throughout my life." (She sleeps?) "We lie awake in love and in fear, in turmoil and in tears," she wrote. "We stare at walls and drink until they speak back. We twist in our self-made cages and pray that we aren't—right this minute—about to make some fateful life-altering mistake. This is a collection of music written in the middle of the night, a journey through terrors and sweet dreams."

So many of her obsessions come together on *Midnights*. "Mastermind," "You're on Your Own, Kid," "Bejeweled," "Midnight Rain"—she can't stop building her own lavender labyrinths and getting lost in them. She's too in love with the things that haunt her in the middle of the night. A mastermind brilliant enough to lie awake and keep designing her complex emotional cages. Never brilliant enough to stay out of them.

TAYLOR SET THE SCENE FOR *MIDNIGHTS* WITH SOME SERI-ously twisted photos. She's in a room with a heavy 1970s motel vibe: Wood paneling, sickly green carpet, shaggy curtains, the works. The ashtray. The lighter. The vintage Wurlitzer keyboard. She lounges on the couch with her feet up, listening to some proggy-looking vinyl. This place looks like it got decorated by Carol Brady after a few Harveys Bristol Creams. Nothing good has ever happened in this room.

She dropped *Midnights* ten years (minus one day) after *Red*, in October, the most Swiftian of months. She aired a "teaser trailer" in the third quarter of an NFL game. This was long before her Travis Kelce era, so there was zero crossover—it irritated Saints and Cardinals fans even more than it did *her* fans. Maybe she hoped to start a nationwide dialogue between football fans explaining what a "third-down conversion" is and Swifties explaining the daisy sym-bolism in "You're on Your Own, Kid."

But it was all just her way of making sure *Midnights* got heard in the right state of sleep deprivation, wreaking havoc on fans' adrenal glands. She even scheduled a secret surprise for 3 a.m.: seven more songs, with Aaron Dessner on board for gems like "The Great War" and "Bigger Than the Whole Sky."

"Anti-Hero" sounded like one of her typical lead singles, jokey and self-referential, but became one of her biggest hits. "This song is a real guided tour through all the things I tend to hate about myself," she said on TikTok. She's dressed for revenge, settling scores against men (even if calling the Feds is the opposite of vigilante shit). I hated "Karma" at first, but the chorus snuck up on me over the radio, thanks to Ice Spice. The title might evoke John Lennon or George Harrison, but it's exactly the song Paul McCartney would have written about karma in 1975 to fill out side two of Wings' *Venus and Mars*. "Karma is a cat" is a total Seventies Macca hook, as well as one that makes you picture George Harrison punching a wall.

"Labyrinth" is a favorite that I have never talked anyone else into giving a shit about, but it's perfect for when you want to forget about Taylor the songwriter and just listen to her flex as one of pop's most brilliant vocalists. It's minimal lyrically—she's got choruses with more verbal content than this song. She sighs, "Breathe in, breathe through / Breathe deep, breathe out," over the synth sparkles. (She dropped that line six months earlier, in her speech to the NYU graduates.) Antonoff goes for the sound of Brian Eno circa *Another Green World*, but he also digs deep into Eighties synth cheese, especially the long-lost Miami Sound Machine hit "Falling in Love (Uh-Oh)," from deep in the Gloria Estefan catalog. "Glitch" is a love letter to deep-blue Nineties R & B, with a faux-Babyface hook in that final "must be counterfeit." There's so much of that across *Midnights*, with "Lavender Haze" and "Midnight Rain," where she rejects "the 1950s shit they want from me," where "the only kind of girl they see is a one-night or a wife." (In the same NYU speech, she revealed, "I had a phase where, for the entirety of 2012, I dressed like a 1950s housewife.")

"Snow on the Beach" is the highlight: weird but fucking

beautiful—the ultimate Taylor combination. It's got Quill Pen, Fountain Pen, Glitter Gel Pen—so many Taylors, there's barely any room for Lana Del Rey. (Maybe she sang the commas?) It sounds frivolous at first, even fluffy, except it soars like "Enchanted" and punches like "Clean." It's about feeling weightless, in your own private world, gazing at your own emotional upheavals from a distance. It poses as a cheap cardigan of a song, easy to slip on and off. You don't feel it in your bones right away, like you do with "The Great War" or "Maroon." But then she slides into "blurring out my per-i-pher-y" and you realize you're caught in her trap. Every detail is so fiendishly planned—the harps, the heartbeat buried in the second verse, right up to those beatific final seconds. It's coming down, it's coming down, it's coming down.

FOREVERMORE

S ummer 2023: Taylor Swift is on the road, with her most gigantic tour. I spent three consecutive nights at her New Jersey shows, over Memorial Day weekend in the first flush of another cruel summer, singing and weeping and suffering through an emotional epic Taypocalypse. She keeps building the legend of her Eras Tour, week by week, city by city, making every night so much longer, wilder, louder, more jubilant than it has to be. In 2024, she added the new songs to the set from *The Tortured Poets Department*. She called this section of the show *Female Rage: The Musical*.

I went three nights. Night one was with my old friend Darius, founder of the indie label Jagjaguwar, who was mostly there to see Phoebe Bridgers. He knew only a handful of Swift songs, yet he marveled at the sight—as he said, "She's throwing them raw meat." The next night was in the nosebleeds, a mile in the sky, then up close to the catwalk for Night Three. "There is one thing that I daydream about with the childlike enthusiasm of a hundred birthday parties!" she yelled, and that is MetLife Night One! I got home Friday night at 4 a.m. and sat on my roof, listening to "Getaway Car" and "Maroon" till dawn, watching the sun come up over Brooklyn to "Marjorie," wondering how I was going to steel myself through two more nights.

The sheer bombardment of songs was physically overwhelming—during "All Too Well" everyone was ready to be carried out on a stretcher, only to realize, *We're barely halfway through*. She made it a real "you know you won so what's the point of keeping score?" moment. She sang "The 1" with that extra note, "You meet some woman on the internet and *taaaaake* her *hooome*." She did the bridge of "Illicit Affairs," the "Don't call me 'kid'" chant—a song about sordid meetings in parking lots, just an hour after "Fearless," about a different couple in a different lot, but maybe the same girl a few years down the line. She slipped in her acoustic wild-card songs: Friday she did "Getaway Car" (with Jersey boy Jack Antonoff) and "Maroon"; Saturday had a pair of New York love songs, "Holy Ground" and "False God"; Sunday it was "Welcome to New York" and "Clean."

Evermore hit hardest—truly the most Era of the Eras, the one that transforms most in a live setting, as her moodiest, most introspective songs become stadium bangers, fom the U2 guitar pulse of "'Tis the Damn Season" to the heartache of "Champagne Problems." "Willow" became a goth ritual—the fans next to me said, "This is where she has a séance."

When Phoebe Bridgers joined her to sing "Nothing New," she confessed, "You are my hero," making Taylor groan. Ice Spice joined her for "Karma." It's strange how Eras Tour feels so forward-facing, even as Swift rummages through the past. It's a pop history that's so rich and deep and multilayered, but one she's still rewriting before our eyes.

Her *Eras Tour* movie dropped in October, as euphoric as the concert—especially seeing it in the theater with a rowdy opening-night crowd of hellions. Right as the lights went down, the girl in Row H yelped, "Oh my God, I should have asked permission before now, but we're all gonna sing, right? Because I wanna sing!" The woman in Seat F-3 replied, "Sing loud and proud, sister." And that's all the discussion anyone needed about that. During "The One," when Taylor sang the line, "You know the greatest films of all time were never made," a fan near me yelled, "Until now!"

It said something about her cultural clout that when she announced her movie premiere—Friday the thirteenth, when else—other movies scrambled for cover, even the blockbuster-in-waiting *The Exorcist 2. (The power of Tay compels you.)* I saw it in the East Village, a few blocks north of Cornelia Street, where my ticket cost $19.89. (Kids got in for $13.13.) There were audible whimpers of pain when she sat at her moss-covered piano for "Champagne Problems." For the surprise songs, the film cleverly paired "Our Song" on guitar with "You're on Your Own, Kid" on piano. It felt like the adult Taylor looking back with empathy at the nervous, always trying-too-hard teenage Taylor, the desperate kid she used to be and the kid she knows she's on some level doomed to stay. It's a dialogue across seventeen years, but you can also hear that both of these Taylors speak the same language.

After the credits, as the lights came up, the girls behind me yelled, "Don't go! She's gonna come back out and do 'Haunted'!" I'm still surprised she didn't.

Taylor split with her longtime boyfriend Joe Alwyn in April 2023, and she jumped into a new high-profile match with the Kansas City Chiefs tight end, Travis Kelce. It was novel how ardently he pursued her in public, and how enthusiastically he hammered it up in the role of her beau. It was the first time we'd seen anyone audition so hard to be her boyfriend, as if he'd carefully studied "Betty" and "Our Song" and "How You Get the Girl" for his playbook. She enjoyed being courted, telling *Time*, "This all started when Travis very adorably put me on blast on his podcast, which I thought was metal as hell." But after her six-year "Sweet Nothing" era with Alwyn, she relished the kind of high-profile relationship everyone thought she was over. He had his own money and his own fame—he even starred in his own reality TV dating show in 2016, *Catching Kelce*. When she did "Karma" on the Eras Tour, she sang "Karma is the guy on the Chiefs," where she used to have "the guy on the screen."

She also seemed to love that Kelce was her gold ticket to the NFL, which was a new world for her to conquer—it was probably the last bastion of American culture she hadn't snuck into yet. All those years after singing "Fifteen," she saw the positive side of dating the boy on the football team. When the Chiefs made it to the Super Bowl, she turned the big game into a "Taylor gets up to dance at an award show" party. She huddled with Lana Del Rey, chugged a beer on the Jumbotron, got booed, got cheered, and then joined him on the field after the Chiefs won. The Super Bowl, the most sacrosanct of U.S. sports rituals, became a whole new experience with Taylor in the mix, although whether that's a plus or a minus depended on your gridiron perspective. In my family, where everyone's a Swiftie or a football fan but most of us are both, the Super Bowl snacks menu included delicacies like 'Tis the Damn Cheeseplate, Nacho Problem Anymore, and I Might Be Queso But I'm Not Fundido All.

In February, she announced her new album, made in secret during the Eras tour, in her spare time. True to form, she broke the news in the middle of winning a Grammy. *The Tortured Poets Department* was full of cathartic breakup songs, with the credo, "All's fair in love and poetry." Two hours after it dropped, she added *The Anthology*, another hour of even sadder songs. It all ranged from the disco dazzle of "I Can Do It With a Broken Heart" to the witchy acoustic lament "The Prophecy." Yet Taylor didn't spend much time on her new flame, or the one she'd just spent six years with. Her muse was a rock star, Matty Healy from The 1975. Many fans had forgotten her 2023 Matty fling even happened, but he was the one who made her mad enough to write these tunes. All over the album, they're two poets who only want love if it's torture. In the excellent title song, she rages, "You're not Dylan Thomas / I'm not Patti Smith / This ain't the Chelsea Hotel." It's the small-town teen romance of "White Horse" ("I'm not a princess, this ain't a fairy tale") updated for the big city. (And as Taylor knows, that's where Dylan Thomas drank himself to death at his favorite Greenwich Village bar, which happened to be called the White Horse.) Patti Smith loved it.

"This period of the author's life is now over, the chapter closed and boarded up," the Chelsea Girl posted. "There is nothing to avenge, no scores to settle once wounds have healed. And upon further reflection, a good number of them turned out to be self-inflicted. This writer is of the firm belief that our tears become holy in the form of ink on a page. Once we have spoken our saddest story, we can be free of it . . . And then all that's left is the tortured poetry." Oh yeah, closing the chapter on the past—her specialty. These are eloquent words, yet I prefer how my colleague Brittany Spanos summed it up on Twitter: "i see taylor learned a valuable lesson which is that if a dj didn't ruin your life then god gonna send a tattooed lead singer of a rock band to finish the job every time."

In August, her Vienna shows were cancelled because of a planned terrorist bombing attack. My sisters Tracey and Caroline were there for the shows—one flew in from London, the other from Boston, with their husbands Bryant and John. It was a fearful weekend for me, yet my sisters spent it in the streets, singing with thousands of other Swifties who'd traveled from around the world. The crowds gathered at Singer Strasse and (of course) Cornelius Gasse, trading bracelets, wearing their Eras fits, making friends (a fan from the Czech Republic in her "A Lot of Female Rage Going on at the Moment" shirt), refusing to hide. Everyone sang "All Too Well," "I Can Do It With a Broken Heart," the startlingly apt "Haunted," "Don't Blame Me," "Delicate"—the "1, 2, 3, let's go bitch" chant has never sounded so fierce or so moving. "Wildest Dreams," that one was huge—they sang it four times. "Fearless" has crushed me in so many contexts, but watching my sisters sing it with all these strangers in the streets of Vienna, channeling fear into celebration—the song will never hit me harder than that.

Taylor is now zooming through a new realm of fame. She rarely does interviews anymore, but when she does, she seems to toy with the format, as if to amuse herself, like when *Time* named her the 2023 "Person of the Year." Thus spake Taylor: "I'm collecting horcruxes. I'm collecting infinity stones. Gandalf's voice is in my head every time I put out a new one. For me, it is a movie now." How do you even interpret this? To a journalist's perspective, it translates as "I could say literally anything and there is zero chance this interviewer will ask what the hell I'm talking about." David Bowie had to spend the Seventies gobbling Bolivia through his face before he started talking this way.

She always worried about fading before her time. She turned twenty-two at the end of 2011, a couple of weeks after I saw her live for the first time. She'd already written a song about the birthday for her next album, *Red*. "Nothing New," she called it. But she didn't release it for another decade. She explored her fear that the audience would fall out of love with her, after she wasn't an ingenue anymore. She asks, "How can a person know everything at eighteen, but nothing at twenty-two? And will you still want me when I'm nothing new?" It's the total opposite of the pop firecracker she puts on the album, where she exulted, "I don't know about you, but I'm feelin' twenty-two!" Nobody heard "Nothing New" until *Red (Taylor's Version)* in 2021, when she was feelin' thirty-two, singing it as a duet with Phoebe Bridgers. But in November 2011, Phoebe was a teenager in Pasadena, California, who got the idea to write her own songs when she heard Taylor Swift on the radio. Taylor helped create a world where her songs would live on, even while she's still in a frenzy writing new ones. Just like Phoebe Bridgers said: *The World (Taylor's Version)*.

ACKNOWLEDGMENTS

Thank you to everyone who has helped me. Carrie Thornton is the mastermind whose wisdom and inspiration shines on every page of this book, as it does in all my books, as my editor and guru. Sharing music with her over the years is one of the deepest joys in my life. Thanks, Carrie.

I'm deeply grateful to all the ferocious team at Dey Street Books, especially Drew Henry, Eliza Rosenberry, Kelly Cronin, Mark Robinson, Allison Carney, Heidi Richter, Cliff Haley, Ben Steinberg, Ronnie Kutys, Emily Metzger, Mary Interdonati, Megan Traynor, Jessica Lyons, Megan Carr, and Rachel Berquist. Thanks to you all. My agent Matthew Elblonk has the cerebral depths of *Folklore* and the sparkle of *1989*.

I'm thankful for all the brilliant, passionate, argumentative music fans whose voices are all over this book, especially my friends and family. Thanks to Jenn Pelly for endless insights and screaming along with "The Archer." Brittany Spanos, who teaches the NYU class on Taylor, one of the world's leading experts on her—but what *isn't* she an expert on? Debating Taylor with Brittany and Brian Hiatt on the *Rolling Stone Music Now* podcast has been an education over the years. Thanks for superhuman help from Gavin Edwards, Joe Levy, Andy Greene, Angie Martoccio, Christian Hoard, and Jon Dolan.

I'm grateful to all my colleagues at *Rolling Stone*, past and present, where we argue about Taylor Swift more or less constantly. Sean Woods is forever the maestro. Maria Fontoura, Gus Wenner, Julyssa Lopez, Alison Weinflash, Jason Newman, Lisa Tozzi, Jason Fine, Waiss Aramesh, Larisha Paul, Simon Vozick-Levinson, CT Jones, Maya Georgi, Kory Grow, Leah Luser, Hank Shteamer, Mankaprr Conteh, Jodi Guglielmi, David Browne, Alan Sepinwall, Jonathan Blistein, Joe Hudak, Jonathan Bernstein, David Fear, Andre Gee, Tessa Stuart, Griffin Lotz, and so many more. A toast of three hundred takeout coffees to you all.

Thanks to Tree Paine, queen of the universe, who is not merely the coolest in any room she's in but also the one who is always correct about the Depeche Mode discography. (RIP, Fletch.) Thanks to all the Swiftian scholars around the world who have elucidated this music over the years—special knowledge to Hannah, @sippingaugust, who is always spinning my head around with her insights. Thank you to Sarah Grant and Jillian Grant for barstool wisdom, Darius Van Arman, Kelly Kerrigan, Ilana Kaplan, Lori Majewski, Marc Weidenbaum, Jeffrey Stock, Stephanie Wells and Boots, Suzy Exposito, Erica Tavera, Abbey Bender, Jennifer Ballantyne, Matthew Perpetua, Gabriella Paiella, The Softies, and Safety Tess. Thanks Alan Light and everyone at Housing Works. Here's to the Hold Steady and all who sail with them. Cosmic gratitude to Pier Harrison, Liz Pelly, Jordan Lee, and Jolie M-A.

Thanks to Chuck Klosterman, Brian Clary, Ann Powers, Amanda Petrusich, Lindsay Zoladz, Sean Howe, Katy Krassner, Stacey Anderson, Chris O'Leary, Keith Harris, Brooke Huffman, Jessica Hopper, Joe Gross, Lizzy Goodman, Amanda Poryes, Caroline Sullivan, Tara Giancaspro, Laura Snapes, Caryn Ganz,

Maria Sherman, Aayushmita Bhattacharjee, Bianca in the MetLife Night 1 bus line, Melissa Eltringham, George Rosett, and Megan Oddsen. Salutes to the Holy Swift podcast: Krista Doyle, Kelly Doyle, and Jessica Zaleski. To Brian Mansfield, Chris Willman, Taffy Brodesser-Akner, Robert Christgau, Melissa Maerz, Greil Marcus, Tavi Gevinson. Darcey Steinke, whose Swift connections run from Marguerite Duras to Saint Bernadette. Thank you Paula Erickson. A salute to the gentleman of Duran Duran for their insight.

Forever and always: Mary T. Sheffield and Bob Sheffield.

This book is dedicated to the coolest and loudest Swiftie legends in my life, my beloved nieces and nephews: Maggie, Matthew, Jackie, David, Sydney, Allison, Sarah, and Charlie. I can't even say "I hope you shine" because you're the reason I do. My sisters are the women who make me lucky and I idolize them. Here's to the flawless, truly something, fearless Tracey ("The Best Day") and Bryant ("You Belong With Me") Mackey, Caroline ("Betty") and John ("Exile") Hanlon, Ann ("Blank Space") Sheffield and John ("Mine") Grub. Love to Donna, Joe, Sean, Jake, Rayna, and Elyza Rose. We're a big loud Irish family, we love to argue about music, and you do not want to be near us in a pub when these songs come on, but Taylor Swift's music has kept us fed. Happy are we who are called to her supper. Massive love to all Sheffields, Mackeys, Hanlons, Twomeys, Crists, Polaks, and Needhams.

Most of all, eternal love and gratitude to Ally, forever my new romantic.

ABOUT THE AUTHOR

Rob Sheffield is a longtime writer for *Rolling Stone*, where he has been covering music and pop culture since 1997. He is the author of the national bestsellers *Love Is a Mix Tape: Love and Loss, One Song at a Time*; *Talking to Girls About Duran Duran: One Young Man's Quest for True Love and a Cooler Haircut*; *Turn Around Bright Eyes: A Karaoke Journey of Starting Over, Falling in Love, and Finding Your Voice*; and *On Bowie*. His book *Dreaming the Beatles: The Love Story of One Band and the Whole World* won the 2017 Virgil Thomson Award for Outstanding Music Criticism. He lives in Brooklyn and will ruin your karaoke night with "Enchanted."